THE PHILOSOPHY
OF
THE TEACHINGS
OF ISLAM

By

**Hadhrat Mirza Ghulam Ahmad
of Qadian**
The Founder of the Ahmadiyya Movement in Islam

Translated into English by
Sir Muhammad Zafrulla Khan
(former Foreign Minister of Pakistan, President of the U.N. General
Assembly & The International Court of Justice at The Hague)

1996
Islam International Publications Ltd.

The Philosophy of the Teachings of Islam
by: Hadhrat Mirza Ghulam Ahmad of Qadian

First published in U.K. by:
The London Mosque in 1979 (50,000)
Reprinted by:
Islam International Publications Ltd. in 1989 (10,000)
Reprinted in U.K. in 1992 (10,000).
Present edition in U.K. in 1996 (51,000)

Published by:
Islam International Publications Ltd.,
'Islamabad', Sheephatch Lane
Tilford, Surrey GU10 2AQ U.K.

Printed in U.K. by Unwin Brothers Limited
The Gresham Press, Old Woking, Surrey

British Library Cataloguing in Publication data
Ahmad, Mirza Ghulam, *1835-1908*
The philosophy of the teachings of Islam.
1. Ahmadiyyat
I. Title
297'. 2046

ISBN 1-85372-193-X
ISBN 1-85372-198-0 Pbk

PUBLISHER'S NOTE

"The Philosophy of the Teachings of Islam" is a well known essay on Islam by Hadhrat Mirza Ghulam Ahmad, Founder of the Ahmadiyya Movement in Islam. The original was written in order to be read at a Conference of Great Religions held at Lahore on December 26-29, 1896. It has since served as an introduction to Islam for seekers of religious knowledge and truth in different parts of the world. It deals with the following five broad themes set by the moderators of the Conference: (i) The physical, moral and spiritual states of man (ii) what is the state of man after death? (iii) the object of man's life and the means of its attainment (iv) the operation of the practical ordinances of the Law in this life and the next and (v) sources of Divine knowledge.

It has been published widely in several languages in different countries. The present revised edition was translated by the late Sir Muhammad Zafrulla Khan with meticulous care and faithfulness to the original text which was lacking in previous English translations.

Quranic references herein cite chapter and verse. In some renderings, the opening verse (ie: *"Bismillah Al-Rahman Al-Rahim"* - In the name of Allah - the Gracious - the Merciful) is not counted and readers using such editions should keep this point in mind to obtain the relevant reference.

Table of Contents

A Message from
Hadhrat Mirza Tahir Ahmad,
Head of the World-wide Ahmadiyya Muslim Community

The World-wide Ahmadiyya Muslim Community is celebrating one hundred years of the publication of this outstanding work, which was originally presented at a conference of religions held in Lahore on December 26-29, 1896. This treatise was written under Divine blessings and its singular success was vouched with prophetic revelations from God, which were published before the conference was conducted. Also hand bills and posters were displayed in many public places in Lahore .

As behoves a community of believers, our celebration of thanksgiving is meaningful and dignified and is free from every kind of useless and trivial display and exultation. We are therefore celebrating the centenary of this book by translating it into most major languages. We hope its blessings will thus be widely shared by most nations of the world.

By the sheer grace of God we have, so far, completed the translation and publication of this book into fifty two major languages of the world. In addition, translation into some of the remaining languages is also in progress; we expect that, with the grace of God, these will be complete before the end of the year 1996.

May Allah reward those who have dedicated their potential, time and effort for the realisation of this noble task. Amen.

Mirza Tahir Ahmad
January 1996.

Introduction

A person by the name of Swami Sadhu Shugan Chandra had spent three or four years of his life attempting to reform the Kaaisth Hindu caste. In l 892 he came to the conclusion that unless people were gathered together under one roof, his efforts would be in vain. He therefore proposed to convene a religious conference, with the first one taking place in 1892 in Ajmer. In 1896, considering Lahore to be a suitable venue, he began preparations for the second such religious conference Swami Sahib appointed a committee to oversee the arrangements. Master Durgah Parshad was president of the committee, and Lala Dhanpat Roy, BA, LLB, its chief secretary. The dates chosen for the convention were 26-28 December 1896, and the following six people were nominated as its moderators:

I . Roy Bahadur Babu Partol Chand Sahib, Judge Chief Court, Punjab.
2. Khan Bahadur Sheikh Khuda Baksh Sahib, Judge Small Cause Court, Lahore.
3. Roy Bahadur Pandit Radhma Kishan Sahib Cole, Pleader Chief Court Lahore, former governor of Jammu.
4. Hadhrat Maulvi Hakeem Nur-ud-Din Sahib, Royal Physician.
5. Roy Bhavani Das Sahib, MA, Extra Settlement Officer, Jhelum.
6. Sardar Jawahar Singh Sahib, Secretary Khalsa Committee, Lahore.[1]

The committee invited the learned representatives of Muslims, Christians and Aryas to set forth the excellences of their respective faiths. The objective of the Conference of Great Religions, to be held at the Lahore Town Hall, was that the excellences and the

---

1. Report Conference of Great Religions. Page 253, 254 printed by Siddiqi Press, Lahore 1897.

merits of the true religion be espoused in a gathering of cultured people and that its love be instilled in their hearts and that they become well acquainted with its arguments and proofs. The learned divines of every religion would thus be given the opportunity to convince others of the truth of their respective religions, while the listeners would be able to assess each speech in relation to the others and accept the truth from wherever it was to be found.

Disputes between the followers of different religions have given rise to the desire to seek the true faith. This is best achieved by bringing together the learned preachers and teachers so that they may, in the context of a few published questions, set forth the beauties of their respective faiths. In such a conference, the true religion from God will definitely become patent.

This is the objective of the conference. Every learned teacher and preacher knows that he is duty-bound to make evident the verities of his faith. The conference is being held so that the truth may become manifest and it is thus a God-given opportunity for them (the learned divines) to fulfil this objective. Such opportunities are not always available to us.

Prevailing upon them further, Swami Sahib wrote:

> If a person sees another suffering from a fatal disease, and he firmly believes that he   holds the cure for the disease, and he also claims to have sympathy for the human race, then how is it possible for him to intentionally turn away when called upon to provide a remedy? My heart is filled with the desire to know which religion is the one replete with truth. I have not the words to express my fervour.

Representatives of various religions accepted Swami Sahib's invitation, and the Conference of Great Religions was held during the Christmas holidays of 1896. Each of the speakers was required to address five questions published in advance by the committee.

ii

The committee also stipulated that, as far as possible, each speaker should confine his answers to the holy book of his religion.

The questions were:

1. The physical, moral and spiritual states of man.
2. What is the state of man after death, i.e. the hereafter?
3. What is the true purpose of man's existence on earth and how can it be achieved?
4. What are the affects of one's deeds in this life and the after life?
5. What are the sources of divine knowledge?

The conference was held on 26-29 December and was attended by representatives of Sanatan Dharm, Hinduism, Arya Samaj, Free Thinker, Brahmo Samaj, Theosophical Society, Religion of Harmony, Christianity, Islam and Sikhism. All representatives addressed the conference, but only one of the lectures provided a true and complete answer to all five questions.

Words cannot describe the atmosphere of the conference when Maulvi Abdul Karim Sialkoti, most eloquently, delivered the lecture. Every person, regardless of religion, could not help but show his appreciation and approbation. There was not one person who was not engrossed and enraptured. The style of delivery was most interesting and appealing. What better proof of the lecture's excellence than the fact that even the opponents were full of praise for it. Despite being a Christian newspaper, the Civil and Military Gazette, Lahore, considered this speech to be the only one worthy of mention and it was the only one which it commended highly.

The speech was written by Mirza Ghulam Ahmad of Qadian, founder of the Ahmadiyya Muslim Community. It could not be completed in the two hours allocated for it, so the conference had to be extended for an extra day. The newspaper Punjab Observer filled column after column with applause for it. Paisa Akhbar, Chaudhvin Sadee, Sadiq-ul-Akhbaar, Mukhbir I Dakkan and General-o-Gohari

Asifi of Calcutta etc. all these newspapers were unanimous in their acclaim. Non-Muslims and non-Indians all declared the essay to be the most superior one of the conference.

The secretary of the conference, Dhanpat Roy, BA, LLB, Pleader Chief Court, Punjab, wrote in his 'Report of the Conference of Great Religions' (Dharam Mohotsu):

> There was an interval of half an hour following the speech of Pandit Gordhan Das Sahib. As the next item on the agenda was a speech presented on behalf of a renowned advocate of Islam, most people did not leave their place. The large Islamia College building began to fill up long before 1.30pm. The gathering numbered between seven and eight thousand people. Educated and knowledgeable people from various religions and nations were present and although plenty of tables, chairs and floor space had been provided, still hundreds of attendees were left with no choice but to stand. The attendees included many dignitaries, Leaders from Punjab, scholars, barristers, lawyers, professors, extra assistants and doctors. In short, different branches of educated society were all present. They stood for four to five hours listening with great patience and with rapt attention and this shows how deeply they cared for this sacred cause. The writer of the paper did not attend in person, but one of his disciples, Maulvi Abdul Karim Sialkoti, was delegated to read it at the conference. The committee had allotted two hours for the essay; however it was not finished in this time. Seeing the avid interest shown by the audience, the moderators willingly agreed to extend the session until the conclusion of the speech. This decision was in exact keeping with the wishes of the participants. Maulvi Abu Yusuf Mubarak Ali agreed to forgo his time so that

Mirza Sahib's essay could be concluded. This was widely appreciated by the audience and the moderators. The conference had been due to end at 4.30 p.m., but in view of the wishes of the audience it was extended to beyond 5.30 p.m. The essay was delivered in four hours and from start to finish it was most interesting and well appreciated.

After receiving prophetic revelation from God, on the 21st of December 1896, a few days before the conference, the founder of the Ahmadiyya Movement publicly declared that his essay would be the most overpowering one. A translation of his declaration is presented below:

A Grand Piece of News for Seekers after Truth

[2]In the conference of Great Religions which will be held in Lahore Town Hall on the 26th, 27th and 28th of December 1896, a paper written by this humble one, dealing with the excellences and miracles of the Holy Quran, will be read out. This paper is not the result of ordinary human effort but is a sign among the signs of God, written with His special support. It sets forth the beauties and truths of the Holy Quran and establishes like the noon-day sun that the Holy Quran is in truth God's own Word and is a book revealed by

---

2 In his announcement Swami Shugan Chandra Sahib has invited the leading divines of Muslims, Christians and Aryas, in the name of God, to set forth the excellences of their respective faiths in the conference proposed by him. We wish to inform Swami Sahib that to do honour to the name of God, as mentioned by him, we are ready to comply with his request and, if God so wills, our paper will be read in the proposed conference. Islam is a faith which directs a true Muslim to demonstrate perfect obedience when he is called upon to do something in the name of God. We shall now see how much regard his brothers the Aryas and Christian divines have for the honour of Parmeshwar or for Jesus and whether they are ready to participate in the conference which is to be held in the name of the Glorious Holy One.

the Lord of all creation. Everyone who listens to this paper from the beginning to the end, to my treatment of all the five themes prescribed for the conference, will, I am sure, develop a new faith and will perceive a new light shining within himself and will acquire a comprehensive commentary on the Holy Word of God. This paper of mine is free from human weakness, empty boasts and vain assertions.

I have been moved by sympathy for my fellow human beings to make this announcement, so that they should witness the beauty of the Holy Quran and should realise how mistaken are our opponents in that they love darkness and hate light. God, the All-Knowing, has revealed to me that my paper will be declared supreme over all other papers. It is full of the light of truth, wisdom and understanding which will put to shame all other parties, provided they attend the conference and listen to it from beginning to end. They will not be able to match these qualities from their scriptures, whether they are Christians or Aryas or those of Sanatan Dharm or any others, because God Almighty has determined that the glory of His Holy Book shall be manifested on that day. I saw in a vision that out of the unseen a hand was laid on my mansion and by the touch of that hand a shining light emerged from the mansion and spread in all directions. It also illumined my hands. Thereupon someone who was standing by me proclaimed in a loud voice: *Allahu Akbar, Kharibat Khaibar* (God is Great, Khaibar has fallen). The interpretation is that by my mansion is meant my heart on which the heavenly light of the verities of the Holy Quran is descending, and by Khaibar are meant all the perverted religions which are afflicted with paganism and falsehood, in which man has been raised to occupy the place of God, or in which divine attributes have been cast down from their perfect station. It was thus disclosed to me that the wide publication of this paper would expose the untruth of false religions and the truth of the Quran will spread progressively around the earth till it arrives at its climax. From this vision my mind moved towards the reception of revelation and I received the revelation:

God is with you, and God stands where you stand. this is a metaphor conveying the assurances of Divine support.

I need write no more. I urge everyone to attend the conference in Lahore even at some inconvenience and listen to these verities. If they do so their reason and their faith will derive such benefit as is beyond their expectation. Peace be upon those who follow the guidance.

Ghulam Ahmad
Qadian, 21 December 1896.

It would be appropriate here to present, as a sample, the opinions of a few of the newspapers of the time:

Civil and Military Gazette, Lahore
The participants at the conference showed great interest in the lecture of Mirza Ghulam Ahmad of Qadian. His paper was an expert and flawless defence of Islam, a great number of people belonging to all sections of society came from far and wide to hear it. Mirza Sahib was unable to attend in person, so his essay was read out by a most able student of his, Maulvi Abdul Karim Sialkoti. On the 27th of December he spent three hours on the speech and it was very well received by the attentive audience. However, in the three hours he was only able to cover one of the five questions. Maulvi Abdul Karim promised that if given more time, he would continue with the lecture. The organisers and president therefore decided to extend the conference by an extra day. (Gist)

Chaudhvin Sadee, Rawalpindi
1 February 1897.
By far the best lecture at the conference was the one written by Mirza Ghulam Ahmad and read, in a most beautiful manner, by the

renowned and eloquent speaker, Maulvi Abdul Karim Sialkoti. The lecture was delivered in a total of six hours; four hours on the 27th of December and two hours on the 29th, and it filled one hundred pages. The audience was captivated, every sentence met with applause. At times the audience requested that sentences be repeated over and over again. We have never before heard such a pleasing lecture. In truth, the representatives of the other religions did not address the questions posed by the conference. Most speakers dealt largely with the fourth question, only briefly passing over the other ones. A majority of the speakers talked much but said little. The exception was Mirza Sahib's paper, which gave a detailed and comprehensive answer to each of the individual questions. The audience listened with great interest and with undivided attention to a lecture which they found to be most superior and outstanding.

We are not followers of Mirza Sahib nor do we have any kind of contact with him. However we cannot be unjust in our commentary. In answering the questions, Mirza Sahib relied solely on the Quran. Every major Islamic principle was beautifully expounded using logical and convincing arguments. To first use logical arguments to prove the existence of God and to then quote the Word of God is style which we find most charming. Not only did Mirza Sahib expound on the philosophy of Quranic teachings, he also explained the philosophy and philology of the Quranic language. In short, Mirza Sahib's lecture was complete and comprehensive, replete with gems of knowledge, wisdom, truths and mysteries. The philosophy of the Divine was so marvellously expressed that the entire audience was left nonplussed. His lecture was the best attended with the hall being packed from top to bottom.

The entire audience listened attentively. To illustrate the difference between Mirza Sahib's lecture and those of other speakers, it would suffice to say that people flocked to hear his paper while, out of boredom, they deserted the others. Maulvi Muhammad Hussain Batalvi's lecture was poor. It was nothing but the usual banal mullahisms, there was nothing exceptional about it. Many people left during Maulvi Mausoof's second lecture and Maulvi Mamduh was not given even a few minutes extra to complete his speech. (Gist)

General-o-Gohar Asifi, Calcutta
24 January 1897.

(The following article was published under the dual title of 'The Conference of Great Religions' and 'The Victory of Islam').

Before discussing the conference in general, we would like to point out that (as our readers know) we have in previous editions already argued as to which learned divine presented the most powerful case on behalf of Islam. Keeping a fair and open mind, one of our distinguished correspondents elected Mirza Ghulam Ahmad of Qadian as the champion of Islam and another correspondent, in a letter to us, has expressed the same opinion. Maulvi Fakhruddin Sahib Fakhr strongly argues that Mirza Ghulam Ahmad of Qadian heads the list, followed by Sir Syed Ahmad Sahib of Aligarh. The other names he suggested as possible champions of Islam were: Maulvi Abu Saeed Muhammad Hussain Sahib Batalvi, Haji Syed Muhammad Ali Sahib Kanpuri and Maulvi Ahmad Hussain Sahib Azeemabadi. It would not be out of place to mention here that one of our correspondents also suggested the name of Maulvi Abdul Haq Sahib Delhvi, author of Tafseer-i-Haqqani. (Gist)

(After publishing an excerpt from Swami Shugan Chandra's invitation to the conference, the newspaper went on to say):

Having read the pamphlets publicising the conference, which of the scholars' sense of pride was awoken to champion the holy religion of Islam? How far did they take up the cause and impress upon others, by way of logical reasoning, the majesty of the Divine?

We have learnt from reliable sources that the organisers of the conference wrote letters of invitation to Mirza Ghulam Ahmad Sahib and Sir Syed Ahmad Sahib. Poor health prevented Hadhrat Mirza

Sahib from attending in person, but he delegated one of his top disciples, Maulvi Abdul Karim Sialkoti, to read his paper at the conference. However Sir Syed did not attend nor did he submit a paper and it was not old-age or other commitments which prevented him from doing so. In fact he considered religious conferences to be unworthy of his attention. In responding to the invitation, (we will publish his response in one of our future editions) he wrote, 'I am not a preacher or a reformer or a maulvi. This conference is for preachers and reformers.' Maulvi Syed Muhammad Ali Sahib Kanpuri, Maulvi Abdul Haq Sahib Delhvi, and Maulvi Ahmad Hussain Sahib Azeemabadi did not show much interest in the conference, and not one of the multitude of other learned, religious scholars of our country bothered to prepare any paper for presentation there. Admittedly, one or two people did take up the challenge, only to see their efforts rebound on themselves. As our next report will prove, they either said nothing relevant or they just made a few empty remarks. The proceedings of the conference show that it was only Hadhrat Mirza Ghulam Ahmad of Qadian who truly championed the cause of Islam and that he honoured the trust people had put in himself for the representation of Islam. His representation was approved by many sects of Islam from Peshawar, Rawalpindi, Jhelum, Shahpur, Bhera, Khushab, Sialkot, Jammoon, Wazeerabad, Lahore, Amritsar, Gurdaspur, Ludhiyana, Shimla, Dehli, Ambala, Riasat Patiala, Dera Doon, Ilahabad, Madras, Bombay, Hyderabad-Dakkan and Bangalore etc... of India.

It is true to say that if Mirza Sahib's paper had not been presented, the Muslims would have been disgraced in comparison to other religions. Had it not been for the powerful hand of the Almighty, the religion of Islam would not have prevailed. It was because of Mirza Sahib's essay that Islam's glory was established. Friends and opponents alike admitted the superiority of the paper over others. In fact, once it was over even the enemies of Islam were forced to admit that the speech had helped them to understand the teachings of Islam and that Islam had been victorious. Mirza Sahib's selection as champion of Islam is most appropriate; no-one can object to his selection He has given us reason to feel proud and in this, is Islam's glory and greatness.

This was only the second Conference of Great Religions, but the size of the gathering and its high intellectual content far surpassed all other congresses and conferences. Great leaders from all the major cities of India were present and we take pride in saying that the city of Madras was also represented. The conference proved to be so interesting that instead of the advertised three days the organisers had to extend it to four days. The organisers had selected Islamia College as the venue as it was the largest public place in Lahore. But so many people participated that even this huge place proved inadequate. The great success of the conference can be seen from the fact that not only did the leading citizens of the Punjab attend, but the judges of the Chief Court and High Court of Allahabad, the honourable Babu Partol Chand Sahib and Mr Bannerji, were also present.

(End of the gist of Newspaper Reports)

Hadhrat Mirza Ghulam Ahmad Sahib's paper was published in *"The Report of the Conference of great Religions"* Lahore and the Ahmadiyya Muslim Community has published it in book form under the title of 'Islami Usool ki Philosophy'. It has been translated into English under the title of 'The Philosophy of the Teachings of Islam'. Many editions of the book have been printed and it has been translated into French, Dutch, Spanish, Arabic, German and various other languages. Many philosophers and foreign newspapers have given it favourable reviews and many Western intellectuals have praised it highly. For example:

1.   **The Bristol Times and Mirror** wrote: 'Surely the man who addresses Europe and America in this manner can be no ordinary being.'(Gist)

2. **Spiritual Journal, Boston** wrote: 'This book is good news for the whole human race.'(Gist)
3. **Theosophical Booknotes** wrote: 'This book is a most beautiful and endearing picture of Muhammad's religion.'(Gist)
4. **Indian Review** wrote: 'This book presents clear thinking and perfect wisdom and the reader is left with no choice but to praise it.'(Gist)
5. **Muslim Review** wrote: 'Anyone reading this book is bound to find a great many truths most deep and pleasing to the soul.'(Gist)

The beauty of the paper is that it does not attack any religion, it only explains the beauty and the merits of Islam. All the questions are answered with reference to the Holy Quran in a manner which proves the perfection of Islam and its superiority over all other religions.

Jalal-ud-Din Shams

A GRAND PIECE OF NEWS FOR SEEKERS AFTER TRUTH

In his announcement Swami Shugan Chandra Sahib has invited the leading divines of Muslims, Christians and Aryas, in the name of God, that they should set forth the excellences of their respective faiths in the Conference proposed by him. We wish to inform Swami Sahib that to do honour to the name of God, as mentioned by him, we are ready to comply with his request and, if God so wills, our paper will be read in the proposed Conference. Islam is a faith which directs a true Muslim to demonstrate perfect obedience when he is called upon to do something in the name of God. We shall now see how much regard his brothers, the Aryas and the Christian divines, have for the honour of Permeshwar or for Jesus and whether they are ready to participate in the Conference which is to be held in the name of the Glorious Holy One.

In the Conference of Great Religions which will be held in Lahore Town Hall on the 26th, 27th and 28th of December 1896, a paper written by this humble one, dealing with the excellences and miracles of the Holy Quran, will be read out. This paper is not the result of ordinary human effort but is a sign among the signs of God, written with His special support. It sets forth the beauties and truths of the Holy Quran and establishes like the noon-day sun that the Holy Quran is in truth God's own Word and is a Book revealed by the Lord of all creation. Everyone who listens to this paper from beginning to the end, to my treatment of all the five themes prescribed for the Conference, will, I am sure, develop a new faith and will perceive a new light shining within himself and will acquire a comprehensive commentary on the Holy Word of God. This paper of mine is free from human weaknesses, empty boasts and vain assertions.

I have been moved by sympathy for my fellow beings to make this announcement, so that they should witness the beauty of the Holy Quran and should realize how mistaken are our opponents in that they love darkness and hate light. God, the All-

Knowing, has revealed to me that my paper will be declared supreme over all other papers. It is full of the light of truth, wisdom and understanding which will put to shame all other parties, provided they attend the Conference and listen to it from beginning to end. They will not be able to match these qualities from their scriptures, whether they are Christians or Aryas or those of Sanatan Dharm or any others, because God Almighty has determined that the glory of His Holy Book shall be manifested on that day. I saw in a vision that out of the unseen a hand was laid on my mansion and by the touch of that hand a shining light emerged from the mansion and spread itself in all directions. It also illumined my hands. Thereupon someone who was standing by me proclaimed in a loud voice: *Allahu Akbar, Kharibat Khaibar* (God is Great, Khaibar has fallen). The interpretation is that by my mansion is meant my heart on which the heavenly light of the verities of the Holy Quran is descending, and by Khaibar are meant all the perverted religions which are afflicted with paganism and falsehood, in which man has been raised to occupy the place of God, or in which divine attributes have been cast down from their perfect station. It was thus disclosed to me that the wide publication of this paper would expose the untruth of false religions and the truth of the Quran will spread progressively around the earth till it arrives at its climax. From this vision my mind moved towards the reception of revelation and I received the revelation (Arabic) God is with you, and God stands where you stand. This is a metaphor conveying the assurance of Divine support.

I need write no more. I urge everyone to attend the Conference in Lahore even at some inconvenience and to listen to these verities. If they do so their reason and their faith will derive such benefit as is beyond their expectation. Peace be upon those who follow the guidance.

Ghulam Ahmad,
Qadian, 21 December 1896.

In the name of Allah, Most Gracious, Ever Merciful.
We praise Him and call down His blessings on His Noble Messenger.

ISLAM

It is necessary that a claim and the reasons in support of it must be set forth from a revealed book.

In this auspicious Conference the purpose of which is that those who have been invited to participate in it should expound the merits of their respective religions with reference to the questions that have been formulated, I shall today set forth the merits of Islam. Before I proceed to do so I deem it proper to announce that I have made it obligatory upon myself that whatever I state will be based upon the Holy Quran which is the Word of God Almighty. I consider it essential that everyone who follows a book, believing it to be revealed, should base his exposition upon that book and should not so extend the scope of his advocacy of his faith as if he is compiling a new book. As it is my purpose today to establish the merits of the Holy Quran and to demonstrate its excellence, it is incumbent upon me not to state anything which is not comprehended in the Quran and to set forth everything on the basis of its verses and in accord with their meaning and that which might be inferred from them, so that those attending the Conference should encounter no difficulty in carrying out a comparison between the teachings of different religions. As all those who believe in a revealed book will also confine themselves to statements comprised in their respective revealed books, I shall not make any reference to the traditions of the Holy Prophet, inasmuch as all true traditions are only derived from the Holy Quran which is a perfect book comprehending all other books. In short this is the day of the manifestation of the glory of the Holy Quran and I humbly beseech God Almighty to assist me in this undertaking. Amen.

FIRST QUESTION

The Physical, Moral and Spiritual States of Man

In the first few pages of this paper I have set forth certain introductory matters which might at first sight seem irrelevant, and yet it is necessary to have a clear concept of those matters for the proper appreciation of the reply to the question that has been set out above.

Three types of human actions

The first question relates to the natural and moral and spiritual states of man. The Holy Quran has indicated three separate sources of these three states. In other words, it has pointed out three springs out of which these respective states flow.

First source; The Self that incites to Evil

The first spring which is the source of all natural states is designated by the Holy Quran the *Nafse Ammarah*, which means *the self that incites to evil*, as it says:

اِنَّ النَّفْسَ لَاَمَّارَةٌ بِالسُّوْءِ (يوسف : ٥٤)

This means that it is characteristic of the human self that it incites man to evil and is opposed to his attainment of perfection and to his moral state, and urges him towards undesirable and evil ways. Thus the propensity towards evil and intemperance is a human state which predominates over the mind of a person before he enters upon the moral state. This is man's natural state, so long as he is not guided by reason and understanding but follows his natural bent in eating, drinking, sleeping, waking, anger and provocation, like the animals. When a person is guided by reason and understanding and brings his natural state under control and regulates it in a proper manner, then these three states, as described, cease to remain the categories as natural states, but are called moral states.

Second source; The Reproving Self
The source of the moral state of man is designated by the Holy Quran *Nafse Lawwama*, as is said:

$$وَلَآ أُقْسِمُ بِالنَّفْسِ الْلَّوَّامَةِ (القيامة:٣)$$

I call to witness the reproving self (75:3); that is to say, I call to witness the self that reproves itself for every vice and intemperance. This reproving self is the second source of human state from which the moral state is generated. At this stage man ceases to resemble the animals. Calling it to witness is for the purpose of doing it honour, as if by advancing from the state of the self that is prone to evil and arriving at the state of the reproving self, it has become worthy of honour in divine estimation. It is so called as it reproves man on vice and is not reconciled to man's submitting to his natural desires and leading an unbridled existence like the animals. It desires that man should be in a good state and should practise good morals, and no kind of intemperance should be manifested in any aspect of human life, and natural emotions and desires should be regulated by reason. As it reproves every vicious movement, it is called the reproving self. Though it reproves itself in respect of vices, yet it is not fully effective in practising virtue and occasionally it is dominated by natural emotions, when it stumbles and falls. It is like a weak child who does not wish to stumble and fall but does so out of weakness, and is then remorseful over his infirmity. In short, this is the moral state of human self when it seeks to comprehend within itself high moral qualities and is disgusted with disobedience, but cannot achieve complete success.

The Third source; The Soul at Rest

The third source which should be described as the beginning of the spiritual state of man is called by the Holy Quran *Nafse Mutmainnah*, that is to say, the soul at rest, as is said:

$$يٰٓاَيَّتُهَا النَّفْسُ الْمُطْمَئِنَّةُ ارْجِعِیْۤ اِلٰی رَبِّكِ رَاضِيَةً مَّرْضِيَّةً$$

$$فَادْخُلِیْ فِیْ عِبَادِیْ وَ ادْخُلِیْ جَنَّتِیْ ۔ رالفجر: ۲۸ ۔ ۳۱)$$

O soul at rest that has found comfort in God return to thy Lord, thou well pleased with Him and He well pleased with thee. Now join My chosen servants and enter into My garden (89:28-31).

This is the stage when the soul of a person being delivered from all weaknesses is filled with spiritual powers and establishes a relationship with God Almighty without Whose support it cannot exist. As water flowing down from a height, on account of its volume and the absence of any obstruction, rushes with great force, in the same way the soul at rest flows towards God. That is indicated by the divine direction to the soul that has found comfort in God to return to its Lord. It undergoes a great transformation in this very life and is bestowed a paradise while still in this world. As this verse indicates in its direction to such a soul to return to its Lord, it is nourished by its Lord and its love of God becomes its nurture, and it drinks at this fountain of life and is thus delivered from death. This is indicated at another place in the Holy Quran where it is said:

قَدْ اَفْلَحَ مَنْ زَكّٰهَا ـ وَقَدْ خَابَ مَنْ دَسّٰهَا (الشمس: ١٠ـ١١)

He who purifies his soul of earthly passions shall be saved and shall not suffer ruin, but he who is overcome by his earthly passions should despair of life (91:10-11).

In short, these three states may be called the natural, moral and spiritual states of man. As the natural urges of man become very dangerous when they are roused and often destroy the moral and spiritual qualities, they are described in God's Holy Book as the self that incites to evil. It may be asked what is the attitude of the Holy Quran towards the natural state of man, what guidance does it furnish concerning it and how does it seek to control it? The answer is that according to the Holy Quran the natural state of man has a very strong relationship with his moral and spiritual states, so much so that even a person's manner of eating and drinking affects his moral and spiritual states. If the natural state of a person is subjected to the control of the directions of divine law it becomes his moral state and deeply affects his spirituality, as is said that whatever falls into a salt mine is converted into salt. That is why the Holy Quran has laid stress on physical cleanliness and postures, and their regulation in relation to all worship and inner purity and spiritual humility. Reflection confirms that physical conditions deeply affect the soul. For instance, when our eyes are filled with tears, even if the tears are artificially induced, the heart is immediately affected and becomes sorrowful. In the same way, when we begin to laugh, even if the laughter is artificially induced, the heart begins to feel cheerful. It has also been observed that physical prostration in prayer induces humility in the soul. As a contrast when we draw ourselves up physically and strut about with our neck raised and our breast pushed forward, this attitude induces a mood of arrogance and vain glory. These instances establish clearly that physical conditions certainly affect spiritual conditions.

Experience also shows that different types of food affect the intellect and the mind in different ways. For instance, careful observation would disclose that people who refrain altogether from eating meat gradually suffer a decline of the faculty of bravery; they lose courage and thus suffer the loss of a divinely bestowed praiseworthy faculty. This is reinforced by the evidence of the divine law of nature that the herbivorous animals do not possess the same degree of courage as do carnivorous ones. The same applies to birds. Thus there is no doubt that morals are affected by food. Conversely those who are given to a diet consisting mainly of meat and eat very little of greens suffer a decline of meekness and humility. Those who adopt the middle course develop both types of moral qualities. That is why God Almighty has said in the Holy Quran:

$$ كُلُوْا وَاشْرَبُوْا وَلَا تُسْرِفُوْا ـ (الاعراف : ٣٢) $$

Eat and drink but do not be immoderate (7:32); that is to say, eat meat and other foods but do not eat anything to excess, lest your moral state be adversely affected and your health might suffer.

As the soul is affected by physical conduct, in the same way sometimes the soul affects the body. For instance, when a person experiences sorrow his eyes become wet, and a person who feels happy, smiles. All our natural actions like eating, drinking, sleeping, waking, moving about, resting, bathing etc., affect our spiritual condition. Our physical structure is related intimately to our total humanity. If a certain part of the brain is injured, memory is immediately lost. An injury to another part of the brain causes loss of consciousness. Poisonous air affects the body and through it the mind, and the whole inner system, to which the moral impulses are related, is impaired and the unfortunate victim passes out quickly like a madman.

Thus physical injuries disclose that there is a mysterious relationship between the soul and the body which is beyond the ken of man. Reflection shows that the body is the mother of the soul. The soul does not descend from outside into the womb of a pregnant woman. It is a light that is inherent in the sperm which begins to shine forth with the development of the foetus. The Word of God Almighty conveys to us that the soul becomes manifest from the framework that is prepared in the womb from the sperm, as is said in the Holy Quran:

ثُمَّ اَنْشَأْنٰهُ خَلْقًا اٰخَرَ فَتَبٰرَكَ اللّٰهُ اَحْسَنُ الْخٰلِقِیْنَ ۔ (المؤمنون: ۱۵)

Then We develop it into a new creation. So blessed is Allah, the Best of Creators (23:15). This means that God bestows a new creation on the body that is prepared in the womb and that new creation is called the soul. Greatly blessed is God Who has no equal as a creator.

The affirmation that a new creation is manifested from the body is a mystery that reveals the reality of the soul and points to the strong relationship between the soul and the body. We are also instructed thereby that the same philosophy underlies the physical acts and words and movements when they are manifested in the cause of God, that is to say, all these sincere actions are charged with a soul as the sperm is charged with a soul. As the framework of those actions is developed, the soul with which they are charged begins to shine and when that framework becomes complete the soul inside it shines forth in its full manifestation and discloses its spiritual aspect. At that stage those actions become fully alive. This means that when the framework of actions is completed, something shines forth from it suddenly like a flash of lightning. This is the stage concerning which God Almighty says in the Holy Quran:

فَإِذَا سَوَّيْتُهُ وَ نَفَخْتُ فِيهِ مِنْ رُّوحِى فَقَعُوا لَهُ

سِجِدِيْنَ (الحجر ٣٠،)

When I have completed his framework and have set right all his manifestations of glory and have breathed into him My spirit, then fall down in prostration all of you, on his account (15:30). This verse indicates that when the framework of actions is completed, a soul shines forth in it, which God attributes to Himself inasmuch as that framework is completed at the cost of worldly life. Thus the divine light which is dim in the beginning suddenly shines forth, so that on the beholding of this divine manifestation, it becomes incumbent on everyone to fall into prostration and to be drawn to that Light. Everyone perceiving that light falls into prostration and is naturally drawn to it, except Iblis who loves darkness.

The soul is created

It is absolutely true that the soul is a fine light developed inside the body and which is nurtured in the womb. To begin with it is hidden and imperceptible and later it is made manifest. From the very beginning its essence is present in the sperm. It is related to the sperm in a mysterious manner by the design and command and will of God. It is a bright and illumined quality of the sperm. It cannot be said that it is a part of the sperm as matter is part of matter, nor can it be said that it comes from outside or falls upon the earth and gets mixed with the matter of the sperm. It is latent in the sperm as fire is latent in the flint. The Book of God does not mean that the soul descends from heaven as a separate entity or falls upon the earth from the atmosphere and then by chance gets mixed with the sperm and enters the womb with it. There is no basis for such a notion. The law of nature rejects it. We observe daily that thousands of insects infect impure and stale foods and are generated in unwashed wounds. Dirty linen secretes hundreds of lice and all sorts of worms are generated inside a person's stomach. It cannot be said that all these come from outside or can be observed as descending from heaven. The truth is that the soul is developed in the body and this also proves that it is created and is not self-existent.

The second birth of the Soul

The design of the Almighty Who has created the soul from the body with His perfect power appears to be that the second birth of the soul should also take place through the body. The movements of the soul follow the movements of the body. If the body is drawn in a particular direction the soul automatically follows it. It is, therefore, a function of the Book of God to direct itself to the natural state of man: that is why the Holy Quran pays so much attention to the reform of the natural state of man and gives directions with regard to everyone of his actions, his laughing, weeping, eating, clothing, sleeping, speaking, keeping silent, marrying, remaining celibate, walking, standing still, outward cleanliness, bathing, submitting to a discipline in health and in illness etc. It affirms that man's physical condition affects his spiritual condition deeply. I cannot undertake a detailed exposition of all those directions as time is not available for such an undertaking.

Gradual Progress of Man

Reflection on the Holy Word of God discloses that it lays down rules for the reform of the natural condition of man and then lifts him gradually upwards and desires to raise him to the highest spiritual state. First, God desires to teach man the rules of social behaviour like sitting, standing, eating, drinking, talking etc., and thus to deliver him from a state of barbarism and distinguish him from the animals and thus bestow upon him an elementary moral state which might be described as social culture. He then desires to regulate his elementary moral habits so that they should acquire the character of high moral qualities. Both these methods are part of the same process as they are related to the reform of man's natural condition. There is between them a difference only of degree. The All-Wise One has so arranged the moral system that man should be able to rise from a low to a high moral condition.

The third grade of progress is that a person should become wholly devoted to the love of his True Creator and to a winning of His pleasure. The whole of his being should be committed to God. To remind Muslims constantly of this grade their religion has been named Islam, which means to devote oneself wholly to God and to keep nothing back. As God, the Glorious, has said:

بَلَىٰ مَنْ اَسْلَمَ وَجْهَهٗ لِلّٰهِ وَهُوَ مُحْسِنٌ فَلَهٗ اَجْرُهٗ عِنْدَ رَبِّهٖ

وَلَاخَوْفٌ عَلَيْهِمْ وَلَاهُمْ يَحْزَنُوْنَ   (البقرة: ۱۱۳)

قُلْ اِنَّ صَلَاتِیْ وَنُسُکِیْ وَمَحْیَایَ وَمَمَاتِیْ لِلّٰهِ رَبِّ الْعٰلَمِیْنَ لَا شَرِیْكَ

لَهٗ وَبِذٰلِكَ اُمِرْتُ وَاَنَا اَوَّلُ الْمُسْلِمِیْنَ ۔ (الانعام: ۱۷۳-۱۷٤)

وَاَنَّ هٰذَا صِرَاطِیْ مُسْتَقِیْمًا فَاتَّبِعُوْهُ وَلَا تَتَّبِعُوا السُّبُلَ فَتَفَرَّقَ

بِكُمْ عَنْ سَبِیْلِهٖ ۔ (الانعام: ۱۵٤)

قُلْ اِنْ كُنْتُمْ تُحِبُّوْنَ اللّٰهَ فَاتَّبِعُوْنِیْ یُحْبِبْكُمُ اللّٰهُ وَ یَغْفِرْ لَكُمْ

ذُنُوْبَكُمْ وَاللّٰهُ غَفُوْرٌ رَّحِیْمٌ ۔ (اٰل عمران: ۳۲)

Salvation means that a person should commit himself wholly to God, and should offer himself as a sacrifice in the cause of God, and should prove his sincerity not only through his motive but also through righteous conduct. He who so comports himself will have his recompense from God. Such people shall have no fear nor shall they grieve (2:113).

Tell them: My prayer and my sacrifices, my living and my dying are all for the sake of God, Whose providence comprehends everything and Who has no associate. So have I been commanded and I am the foremost of those who fulfil this concept of Islam and offer themselves as a sacrifice in the cause of Allah (6:163-164).

This is My straight path then follow it and do not follow any other path which will lead you away from His path (6:154).

Tell them: If you love God then follow me and walk along my path so that God may love you and forgive you your sins. He is Most Forgiving Ever Merciful (3:32).

Distinction Between the Natural and Moral States and a refutation of the Doctrine of Preservation of Life

I shall now proceed to describe the three states of man. But before I do so, it is necessary for me to voice a reminder that, as indicated in the Holy Word of God Almighty, the natural state of man, the fountain head of which is the self that incites to evil, is not something divorced from his moral state. The Holy Word of God has classified man's natural faculties and desires and urges, as natural conditions. These, when they are consciously regulated and controlled and are brought into action on their proper occasions and places, become moral qualities. In the same way, moral conditions are not entirely distinct from spiritual conditions. When moral conditions develop absolute devotion to God and complete purification of self and, cutting asunder from the world, turn wholly to God and to perfect love and complete devotion and full serenity and satisfaction and complete accord with the Divine will, they become spiritual conditions.

So long as his natural conditions are not converted into moral conditions, man deserves no praise, inasmuch as they are to be found in other animates and even in solids also. In the same way the mere acquisition of moral qualities does not bestow spiritual life upon a person. A person who denies the existence of God can yet exhibit good moral qualities, such as to be humble of heart, to seek peace, to discard evil and not to resist the evil-monger. These are all natural conditions which may be possessed even by an unworthy one who is utterly unacquainted with the fountain-head of salvation and enjoys no part of it. Many animals have a gentle disposition, and can be trained to become wholly peaceful and not to react savagely to chastisement, and yet we cannot call them human, let alone humans of high status. In the same way, a person who is entirely misguided and even suffers from some vices, can exhibit these qualities. It is possible that a person may develop mercy to a degree in which he would not permit himself to kill the germs that might be generated in his wounds, or might be so mindful of preserving life that he may not wish to harm the lice in his hair or the insects that are generated in his stomach and his arteries and his brain. I can believe that a person's mercy might impel him to discard the use of honey as it is procured by the destruction of many lives and by driving the poor bees out of their hives. I can believe that a person may avoid the use of musk as it is the blood of a poor animal and is procured by slaughtering it and separating it from its young. I do not deny that a person might refrain from wearing pearls or silk as both these are procured through the death of worms. I can even understand that a person in pain might refuse to be bled by leeches and might prefer to suffer pain himself rather than desire the death of poor leeches. I can even believe that a person might carry his mercy and regard for life to a degree that he might refuse to drink water in order to spare the germs in the water. I can accept all this, but I cannot accept that these natural conditions can be regarded as moral qualities or that they can serve to wash out the inner impurities which obstruct a person's approach to God. I cannot believe that to become harmless to a degree in which some animals and birds excel man can become the means of the acquisition of a high degree of humanity. Indeed, I consider this attitude as amounting to opposition to the law of nature and inconsistent with the high moral quality of seeking the pleasure of God. It rejects the bounties that nature has bestowed upon us. Spirituality can be achieved only through the use of every moral quality in its proper place and on its proper occasion, and through treading faithfully upon the ways of God and through being wholly devoted to Him. He who becomes truly God's cannot exist without Him. A true seeker after God is like a fish sacrificed by the hand of God and its water is the love of God.

Three Methods of Reform: The Advent of the Holy Prophet at the Time of the Greatest Need

As I have stated, there are three springs from which human states flow, namely, the self that incites to evil, the self that reproves and the soul at rest. There are also three methods of reform. The first is that senseless savages should be taught the elementary social values pertaining to eating, drinking, marriage etc. They should not go about naked nor eat carrion, like dogs, nor practise any other type of wildness. This is an elementary stage of the reform of natural conditions of the type that would have to be adopted, for instance, if it is desired to teach a savage from Port Blair, the elementary ways of human behaviour.

The second method of reform is that when a person has adopted elementary human ways, he may be taught the higher moral qualities and should be instructed to employ his faculties in their proper places and on their proper occasions.

The third method of reform is that those who have acquired high moral qualities should be given a taste of the draught of the love of and union with God.

Our lord and master, the Holy Prophet, peace and blessings of Allah be upon him, was raised at a time when the world had been thoroughly corrupted. As God Almighty has said:

$$\text{ظَهَرَ الْفَسَادُ فِي الْبَرِّ وَالْبَحْرِ - (الروم: ٤٢)}$$

Corruption has spread over land and sea (30:42). This means that the People of the Book, as well as those who had no experience of revelation, had all been corrupted. The purpose of the Holy Quran was to revive the dead, as is said:

$$\text{اِعْلَمُوٓا اَنَّ اللّٰهَ يُحْيِ الْاَرْضَ بَعْدَ مَوْتِهَا - (الحديد: ١٨)}$$

Know that Allah is about to revive the earth after its death (57:18).

At that time the people of Arabia were steeped in barbarism. No social pattern prevailed and they took pride in every type of sin and misconduct. A man married an unlimited number of wives, and they were all addicted to the use of everything unlawful. They considered it lawful to marry their mothers, and that is why God Almighty had to prescribe:

$$\text{حُرِّمَتْ عَلَيْكُمْ اُمَّهٰتُكُمْ - (النِّسَآء: ٢٤)}$$

Your mothers are made unlawful for you (4:24). They ate carrion and some of them were even cannibals. There is not a sin of which they were not guilty. Most of them did not believe in the after life. Many of them denied the existence of God. They killed their female infants with their own hands. They killed orphans and devoured their substance. They had the appearance of human beings but were bereft of reason. They possessed no modesty, no shame, and no self respect. They drank liquor like water. The one among them who indulged indiscriminately in fornication was acknowledged as the chief of his tribe. They were so utterly ignorant that their neighbouring people called them the unlettered ones. At such time and for the reform of such people, our lord and master, the Holy Prophet, peace and blessings of Allah be upon him, appeared in Mecca. This was the time that called for the three types of reform that we have just mentioned. That is why the Holy Quran claims to be more complete and more perfect than all other books of guidance, inasmuch as the other books had not the opportunity of carrying out the three types of reforms which the Holy Quran was designed to carry out. The purpose of the Holy Quran was to elevate savages into men, and then to equip them with moral qualities, and finally raise them to the level of godly persons. The Holy Quran thus comprehends all those three projects.

The True Purpose of the Teachings of the Holy Quran is the Reform of the Three Conditions: Natural Conditions by Regulation become Moral Qualities

Before I embark upon a detailed exposition of the threefold reforms that I have just mentioned, it is necessary to point out that there is no teaching in the Holy Quran which is imposed by compulsion. The whole purpose of the Quran is the three reforms, and all its teachings are directed towards that end. All other directions are the means for the achievement of those reforms. As sometimes a surgeon has to perform an operation in order to restore the patient to normal health, or has to apply an ointment, in the same way the teachings of the Quran, out of sympathy for mankind, have recourse to such means also. The purpose of all Quranic insights and admonitions and directions is to raise man from his natural condition of barbarity to a moral state, and then to lift him from that state to the limitless ocean of spirituality.

We have already stated that natural conditions are not something distinct from moral conditions. When they are regulated and are used on their proper occasions, under the direction of reason, they acquire a moral character. Before they are controlled by reason and understanding they have not the character of moral qualities, but are natural impulses, however much they might resemble moral qualities. For instance, if a dog or lamb displays affection or docility towards its master it would not be described as moral or good-mannered. In the same way a wolf or a tiger would not be described as ill-mannered on account of its wildness. A moral state emerges after reflection and regard for time and occasion come into play. A person who does not exercise reason and deliberation is like a child whose mind and intellect are not yet governed by reason, or is like a madman who has lost his reason and good sense. A child or a mad man sometimes behaves in a manner that has the appearance of moral action, but no sensible person calls such conduct moral, as such conduct does not proceed from good sense and appropriateness, but is a natural reaction to the circumstances. A human infant, as soon as it is born, seeks its mother's breasts, and a chicken, as soon as it is hatched begins to pick up corn. In the same way the spawn of a leech behave like a leech, a baby serpent behaves like a serpent and a tiger cub behaves like a tiger. A human infant begins to exhibit human reactions as soon as it is born and those reactions become more and more remarkable as it begins to grow up. For instance, its weeping becomes louder, and its smiles become laughter, and its gaze becomes more concentrated. At the age of a year or eighteen months it develops another natural trait: it begins to display its pleasure and displeasure through its movements and tries to strike someone or to give something to someone. All these motions are natural impulses. Similarly a barbarian who possesses little human sense is like such an infant and displays natural impulses in his words, actions and

movements and is governed by his natural emotions. Nothing
proceeds from him in consequence of the exercise of his inner
faculties. Whatever surges up from his inside under the operation
of a natural impulse and as a reaction to external stimuli, becomes
manifest. It is possible that his natural impulses that are exhibited
as a reaction to an external stimulus may not all be vicious, and
some might resemble good morals, but they are normally not the
consequences of reasonable reflection and consideration, and
even if they are to some degree so motivated they cannot be
relied upon on account of the domination of natural impulses.

True Morals

In short we cannot attribute true morals to a person who is
subject to natural impulses like animals or infants or the insane,
and who lives more or less like animals. The time of true morals,
whether good or bad, begins when a person's reason becomes
mature and he is able to distinguish between good and bad and
the degree of evil and goodness, and begins to feel sorry when he
misses an opportunity of doing good and is remorseful when he
has done some wrong. This is the second stage of his life which is
designated by the Holy Quran the self that reproves. It should,
however be remembered that casual admoniton is not enough to
lead a barbarian to the stage of the self that reproves. It is
necessary that he should become conscious of the existence of
God to a degree at which he should not consider his creation as
without purpose, so that an understanding of the Divine should
stimulate his true moral qualities. That is why God Almighty has
drawn attention to the need of understanding of the Divine, and
has assured man that every act and moral produces an effect
which brings about spiritual comfort or spiritual pain in this life,
and will be manifested clearly in the hereafter. In short, at the
stage of the self that reproves, a person is bestowed so much of
reason and understanding and good conscience, that he reproves

himself over a wrong done by him and is anxious to do good. That is the stage when a person acquires high moral qualities.

Distinction between *Khalq* (creation) and *Khulq* (morals)

Khalq connotes physical birth and *Khulq* connotes inner birth. As inner birth is perfected through moral development and not merely through the exercise of natural impulses, *Khulq* connotes moral qualities and not natural impulses. It should be pointed out that the common conception that morals merely mean meekness, courtesy and humility is entirely mistaken. The truth is that corresponding to every physical action there is an inner quality which is moral; for instance, a person sheds tears through the eyes and corresponding to that action there is an inner quality which is called tenderness, which takes on the character of a moral quality when, under the control of reason, it is exercised on its proper occasion. In the same way, a person defends himself against the attack of an enemy with his hands, and corresponding to this action there is an inner quality which is called bravery. When this quality is exercised at its proper place and on its proper occasion, it is called a moral quality. Similarly a person sometimes seeks to relieve the oppressed from the oppression of tyrants, or desires to make provision for the indigent and the hungry, or wishes to serve his fellow beings in some other way, and corresponding to such action there is an inner quality which is designated mercy. Sometimes a person punishes a wrongdoer and corresponding to such action there is an inner quality which is called retribution. Sometimes a person does not wish to attack one who attacks him and forbears to take action against a wrongdoer, corresponding to which there is a quality which is called forbearance or endurance. Sometimes a person works with his hands or feet or employs his mind and intellect or his wealth in order to promote the welfare of his fellow beings, corresponding to which there is an inner quality which is called benevolence. Thus, when a person exercises all these qualities on their proper occasions and at their proper places they are called moral qualities. God, the Glorious, has addressed the Holy Prophet, peace and blessings of Allah be upon him, in the words:

$$وَاِنَّكَ لَعَلٰى خُلُقٍ عَظِيْمٍ \_ (القلم، ٥)$$

Thou dost most surely possess high moral excellences (68:5). This means that all high moral qualities such as benevolence, courage, justice, mercy, bountifulness, sincerity, high mindedness etc. were combined in the person of the Holy Prophet. In short all the natural qualities of man as courtesy, modesty, integrity, benevolence, jealousy, steadfastness, chastity, piety, equity, sympathy, bravery, generosity, forbearance, endurance, bountifulness, sincerity, loyalty etc., when they are manifested on their proper occasions under the guidance of reason and reflection would all be accounted moral qualities. In reality they are the natural states and impulses of man and are designated moral qualities when they are exercised deliberately on their proper occasions. A natural characteristic of man is that he desires to make progress and, therefore, through following a true religion and keeping good company and conforming to good teachings he converts his natural impulses into moral qualities. No other animal is invested with this characteristic.

Natural States of Man

We shall now proceed to set forth the first of the three reforms which is inculcated by the Holy Quran and which is related to the natural state of man. This reform relates to what are known as good manners, that is to say, the code that regulates the natural conditions of barbarians, like eating, drinking, marriage, etc., and establishes them at a just level of social values and rescues them from an animal existence. In this context the Holy Quran ordains:

حُرِّمَتْ عَلَيْكُمْ أُمَّهٰتُكُمْ وَبَنٰتُكُمْ وَأَخَوٰتُكُمْ وَعَمّٰتُكُمْ وَخٰلٰتُكُمْ وَبَنٰتُ
الْأَخِ وَبَنٰتُ الْأُخْتِ وَأُمَّهٰتُكُمُ الّٰتِيْ أَرْضَعْنَكُمْ وَأَخَوٰتُكُمْ مِّنَ الرَّضَاعَةِ
وَأُمَّهٰتُ نِسَآئِكُمْ وَرَبَآئِبُكُمُ الّٰتِيْ فِيْ حُجُوْرِكُمْ مِّنْ نِّسَآئِكُمُ الّٰتِيْ
دَخَلْتُمْ بِهِنَّ فَاِنْ لَّمْ تَكُوْنُوْا دَخَلْتُمْ بِهِنَّ فَلَا جُنَاحَ عَلَيْكُمْ وَحَلَآئِلُ
اَبْنَآئِكُمُ الَّذِيْنَ مِنْ اَصْلَابِكُمْ وَاَنْ تَجْمَعُوْا بَيْنَ الْاُخْتَيْنِ اِلَّا مَا قَدْ
سَلَفَ ـ ‏(‏النِّسَآء : ٢٤)‏

لَا يَحِلُّ لَكُمْ اَنْ تَرِثُوا النِّسَآءَ كَرْهًا ـ ‏(‏النِّسَآء:٢٠)‏

وَلَا تَنْكِحُوْا مَا نَكَحَ اٰبَآؤُكُمْ مِّنَ النِّسَآءِ اِلَّا مَا قَدْ سَلَفَ ـ
‏(‏النِّسَآء : ٢٣)‏

اُحِلَّ لَكُمُ الطَّيِّبٰتُ .... وَالْمُحْصَنٰتُ مِنَ الْمُؤْمِنٰتِ وَالْمُحْصَنٰتُ
مِنَ الَّذِيْنَ اُوْتُوا الْكِتٰبَ مِنْ قَبْلِكُمْ اِذَآ اٰتَيْتُمُوْهُنَّ اُجُوْرَهُنَّ
مُحْصِنِيْنَ غَيْرَ مُسٰفِحِيْنَ وَلَا مُتَّخِذِيْ اَخْدَانٍ. ‏(‏الْمَآئدة : ٦)‏

وَلَا تَقْتُلُوْا اَنْفُسَكُمْ ـ ‏(‏النِّسَآء : ٣٠)‏

وَلَا تَقْتُلُوْا اَوْلَادَكُمْ ـ ‏(‏الانعام:١٥٢)‏

لَا تَدْخُلُوْا بُيُوْتًا غَيْرَ بُيُوْتِكُمْ حَتّٰى تَسْتَأْنِسُوْا وَ تُسَلِّمُوْا عَلٰى اَهْلِهَا
.... فَاِنْ لَّمْ تَجِدُوْا فِيْهَآ اَحَدًا فَلَا تَدْخُلُوْهَا حَتّٰى يُؤْذَنَ لَكُمْ وَاِنْ
قِيْلَ لَكُمُ ارْجِعُوْا فَارْجِعُوْا هُوَ اَزْكٰى لَكُمْ ـ ‏(‏النور: ٢٨ - ٢٩)‏

وَاْتُوا الْبُيُوتَ مِنْ اَبْوَابِهَاْ ــ (ر البقرة : ١٩٠)

وَ اِذَا حُيِّيْتُمْ بِتَحِيَّةٍ فَحَيُّوْا بِاَحْسَنَ مِنْهَاْ اَوْرُدُّوْهَاْ ــ (ر النِّسَاء : ٨١)

اِنَّمَا الْخَمْرُ وَالْمَيْسِرُ وَالْاَنْصَابُ وَ الْاَزْلَامُ رِجْسٌ مِّنْ عَمَلِ الشَّيْطٰنِ
فَاجْتَنِبُوْهُ لَعَلَّكُمْ تُفْلِحُوْنَ ــ (ر المائدة : ٩١)

حُرِّمَتْ عَلَيْكُمُ الْمَيْتَةُ وَالدَّمُ وَ لَحْمُ الْخِنْزِيْرِ وَ مَاْ اُهِلَّ لِغَيْرِ اللّٰهِ
بِهِ وَالْمُنْخَنِقَةُ وَالْمَوْقُوْذَةُ وَالْمُتَرَدِّيَةُ وَ النَّطِيْحَةُ وَمَاْ اَكَلَ السَّبُعُ اِلَّا مَا
ذَكَّيْتُمْ وَمَا ذُبِحَ عَلَى النُّصُبِ ــ (ر المَائدة : ٤)

يَسْئَلُوْنَكَ مَاذَاْ اُحِلَّ لَهُمْ قُلْ اُحِلَّ لَكُمُ الطَّيِّبٰتُ ــ (ر المائدة : ٥)

اِذَا قِيْلَ لَكُمْ تَفَسَّحُوْا فِى الْمَجْلِسِ فَافْسَحُوْا يَفْسَحِ اللّٰهُ لَكُمْ وَ
اِذَا قِيْلَ انْشُزُوْا فَانْشُزُوْا ــ (ر المجادلة : ١٢)

كُلُوْا وَاشْرَبُوْا وَ لَا تُسْرِفُوْا ــ (ر الاعراف : ٣٢)

وَقُوْلُوْا قَوْلًا سَدِيْدًا ــ (ر الاحزاب : ٧١)

وَ ثِيَابَكَ فَطَهِّرْ   وَالرُّجْزَ فَاهْجُرْ ــ (ر المدثر : ٥-٦)

وَاقْصِدْ فِى مَشْيِكَ وَاغْضُضْ مِنْ صَوْتِكَ ــ (ر لقمان : ٢٠)

وَتَزَوَّدُوْا فَاِنَّ خَيْرَ الزَّادِ التَّقْوٰى ــ (ر البقرة : ١٩٨)

وَاِنْ كُنْتُمْ جُنُبًا فَاطَّهَّرُوْا ‐رِالمَآئدَة : ٧ ›

وَ فِيْ اَمْوَالِهِمْ حَقٌّ لِّلسَّآئِلِ وَالْمَحْرُوْمِ ‐رِالذّٰريتِ:٢٠ ›

وَاِنْ خِفْتُمْ اَلَّا تُقْسِطُوْا فِي الْيَتٰمٰى فَانْكِحُوْا مَا طَابَ لَكُمْ مِّنَ النِّسَآءِ

مَثْنٰى وَ ثُلٰثَ وَ رُبٰعَ فَاِنْ خِفْتُمْ اَلَّا تَعْدِلُوْا فَوَاحِدَةً . . . . .

وَاٰتُوا النِّسَآءَ صَدُقٰتِهِنَّ نِحْلَةً رِالـنِّسَآء : ٤‐٥›

Forbidden to you are your mothers, and your daughters, and your sisters, and your fathers' sisters, and your mothers' sisters, and the daughters of your brothers, and the daughters of your sisters, and your foster-mothers and your foster-sisters, and the mothers of your wives and your step-daughters by your wives with whom you have consorted, but if you have consorted not with them, it shall be no sin upon you, and the wives of your sons, from your loins. You are also forbidden to join two sisters together in marriage; but what has passed has passed. Surely, Allah is Most Forgiving, Ever Merciful (4:24).

It is not lawful for you to inherit from women against their will (4:20).

It is not lawful for you to marry women whom your fathers had married, except that which happened in the past (4:23).

Lawful for you are chaste believing women and chaste women from among those who were given the Book before you, when you give them their dowers, contracting valid marriages, not committing fornication, nor taking secret paramours (5:6). In the time of ignorance some of the Arabs who were childless permitted their wives to consort with someone else for the purpose of having a child. The Holy Quran forbade this practice. The expression taking secret paramours has reference to this practice. Then it is said: Destroy not yourselves (4:30); and slay not your progeny (6:152). Do not enter houses, other than your own, freely like barbarians, until you have obtained leave, and when you have obtained leave and enter, greet the inmates with the salutation of peace. If you find no one therein, then enter not until leave is given to you. If you are told by the inmates to go back then go back (24:28-29).

Do not enter houses by scaling over their walls; enter them through the doors (2:190).

When you are greeted with a salutation greet with a better salutation (4:87).

Liquor, gambling, idols and divining arrows are but abominations and Satanic devices. So turn wholly away from each one of them (5:91).

Forbidden to you is the flesh of a dead animal, and blood, and the flesh of swine; and that on which the name of someone other than Allah is invoked and the flesh of an animal that has been strangled or is beaten to death or is killed by a fall, or is gored to death, and of which a wild animal has eaten and that which has been slaughtered at an altar, for they are all carrion (5:4). If they ask thee what is lawful for them, tell them: All good things are lawful for you (5:5). Refrain from that which is carrion or resembles carrion or is unclean.

When you are asked to make room for others in your assemblies then hasten to make room so that others might be seated; and when you are asked to rise up, then rise up without delay (58:12). Eat of all that is lawful and wholesome like meat, vegetables and pulses etc. but do not be immoderate in any respect (7:32). Do not talk at random and talk to the point (33:71).

Keep your raiment clean and your bodies and your streets and the places where you sit. Take frequent baths and cultivate the habit of keeping your homes neat and tidy (74:5-6).

Moderate your voice and speak not with a loud voice nor whisper and, except when needed otherwise, walk at a moderate pace, neither too fast nor too slow (31:20).

When you go on a journey, make all preparation and take necessary provisions so as to avoid having to beg (2:198). When you consort with your spouses, purify yourselves by bathing (5:7).

When you eat give out of your food to him who asks and also to dogs and other animals and birds (51:20).

There is no harm in your marrying orphan girls who are under your care, but if you apprehend that you may not be fair in dealing with them because they are orphans, then marry women who have parents and relations to be watchful of them, who would respect you and concerning whom you would be careful. You may marry two or three or four of them provided you can deal equitably with all of them. But if you feel that you may not deal justly between them then marry only one, even if you should feel the need of more than one. The limit of four is imposed lest you should be inclined towards marrying a larger number amounting to hundreds according to your old custom and so that you should not incline towards illicit indulgence. Hand over to your wives their dowers freely (4:4-5).

This is the first reform of the Holy Quran whereby man is raised from his natural state and barbaric ways to the status of a civilized social being. In these teachings there is no mention of the higher moral qualities. They are concerned only with elementary human behaviour. This teaching was needed because the people for whose reform the Holy Prophet, peace and blessings of Allah be upon him, was sent, were in an extreme state of barbarity and it was necessary that they should be taught the elementary rules of social behaviour.

Why is the Flesh of Swine Prohibited

One matter to be kept in mind in this context is that in the very name of this animal, God has indicated the reason for the prohibition of its flesh. The Arabic word for swine is *Khinzeer* which is a compound of *Khanz* and *Ara*, which means: I see it very foul. Thus the very name that God Almighty gave to this animal at the beginning points to its uncleanness. It is a curious coincidence that in Hindi this animal is called *Suar*, which is a compound of *Su* and *Ara*. This also means: I see it very foul. It should not be a matter of surprise that the Arabic word *Su* should have found its way into Hindi. We have established in our book *Minanur Rahman*, that Arabic is the mother of all languages and that many Arabic words are to be found in all languages. Thus *Su* is an Arabic word and its equivalent in Hindi is *bad*. This animal is also called *bad* in Hindi. There is no doubt that at the time when Arabic was the universal language this animal was known in this country by an Arabic name which was synonymous with *Khinzeer*, and so it has continued to this day. It is possible that in Sanskrit this word might have undergone some transformation, but the true word is *Khinzeer* which proclaims its own meaning. It is not necessary to enter into a detailed exposition of the foulness of this animal. Everyone knows that it eats filth and is utterly shameless. Thus the reason for the prohibition of its flesh is obvious, as by the law of nature its flesh would have a foul effect on the body and the soul of one who eats it. As we have already demonstrated food affects a person's soul and there can be no doubt that the flesh of such a foul animal would also be foul. Even in pre-Islamic times, Greek physicians had opined that the flesh of this animal particularly damages the faculty of modesty and fosters shamelessness. The eating of carrion is also prohibited in Islamic law for the same reason; that is to say, it affects the moral qualities adversely and is also harmful to physical health. The blood of an animal that is strangled or is beaten to death remains inside the body of the dead animal and they are all carrion. It is obvious that the blood of such an animal is soon corrupted and corrupts the whole flesh. It is established by recent research that the germs in such blood spread a poisonous corruption in the flesh of the dead animal.

Moral Condition of Man

The second part of Quranic reform is that it regulates the natural conditions in such manner as to convert them into high moral qualities. This is a vast subject. If we were to set it forth in detail this paper would become so lengthy that not one tenth of it could be read out in the allotted time. We must, therefore, confine ourselves to the exposition of a few moral qualities by way of illustration.

Moral qualities fall under two heads. First, those moral qualities that enable a person to discard evil; and, secondly, those moral qualities that enable him to do good. Discarding evil comprehends those qualities through which a person tries that he should do no harm to the property, honour or life of a fellow being by his tongue or his hand or his eyes or by any other organ, nor should he design to do him such harm. The doing of good comprehends all those moral qualities whereby a person tries to benefit a fellow being in respect of his property or honour by his tongue or his hand or his knowledge, or by any other means, or determines to make manifest his glory or honour, or overlooks a wrong that had been done to himself and thus benefits the perpetrator of the wrong by sparing him physical pain or financial imposition, or inflicts such chastisement upon him in respect of the wrong which is in reality a mercy for the wrongdoer.

Moral Qualities Related to the Discarding of Evil

The moral qualities that the true Creator has appointed for the discarding of evil are known by four names in Arabic which has a specific name for all human concepts, behaviours and morals.

The first of these moral qualities is called *Ihsan*, that is to say, chastity. This expression connotes the virtue that is related to the faculty of procreation of men and women. Those men and women would be called chaste who refrain altogether from illicit sex and all approaches to it, the consequence of which is disgrace and humiliation for both parties in this world, and chastisement in the hereafter, and dishonour and grave harm for those related to them. For instance, if a person is guilty of an approach towards the wife of another which, though it does not proceed as far as adultery, yet amounts to its preliminaries, it would become incumbent upon the self-respecting husband of the woman to divorce her on account of her willingness to tolerate such an approach. Her children would also be sadly afflicted. The husband would have to endure all this injury on account of the misconduct of a villain.

It should be remembered that the moral quality of chastity would come into play when a person who possesses the capacity for the compassing of this particular vice restrains himself from indulging in it. If he does not possess that capacity, because he is a minor or is impotent or is a eunuch or has arrived at extreme old age, we cannot give him credit for the moral quality of chastity. He has a natural condition of chastity but, as we have repeatedly pointed out, natural conditions cannot be described as moral qualities. They become moral qualities when they are exercised or become capable of being exercised on their proper occasions, under the control of reason. Therefore, minors and impotent ones and those who deprive themselves in some way of sexual capacity cannot be given credit for this moral quality, though apparently they would be leading chaste lives. In all such cases their chastity would only be a natural condition. As this vice and its preliminaries can be practised by both men and women, the Holy Book of God sets forth directions for both men and women in this context. It says:

قُلْ لِّلْمُؤْمِنِيْنَ يَغُضُّوْا مِنْ اَبْصَارِهِمْ وَيَحْفَظُوْا فُرُوْجَهُمْ ذٰلِكَ اَزْكٰى لَهُمْ

... وَ قُلْ لِّلْمُؤْمِنٰتِ يَغْضُضْنَ مِنْ اَبْصَارِهِنَّ وَيَحْفَظْنَ فُرُوْجَهُنَّ

وَلَا يُبْدِيْنَ زِيْنَتَهُنَّ اِلَّا مَا ظَهَرَ مِنْهَا وَلْيَضْرِبْنَ بِخُمُرِهِنَّ عَلٰى

جُيُوْبِهِنَّ .... وَلَا يَضْرِبْنَ بِاَرْجُلِهِنَّ لِيُعْلَمَ مَا يُخْفِيْنَ مِنْ

زِيْنَتِهِنَّ وَ تُوْبُوْا اِلَى اللهِ جَمِيْعًا اَيُّهَ الْمُؤْمِنُوْنَ لَعَلَّكُمْ تُفْلِحُوْنَ

(النور: ٣١-٣٢)

وَلَا تَقْرَبُوا الزِّنٰى اِنَّهُ كَانَ فَاحِشَةً وَسَاءَ سَبِيْلًا (بنى اسرائيل ٣٣)

وَلْيَسْتَعْفِفِ الَّذِيْنَ لَا يَجِدُوْنَ نِكَاحًا ـ (النور: ٣٤)

وَرَهْبَانِيَّةً اِبْتَدَعُوْهَا مَا كَتَبْنٰهَا عَلَيْهِمْ اِلَّا ابْتِغَاءَ رِضْوَانِ

اللهِ فَمَا رَعَوْهَا حَقَّ رِعَايَتِهَا ـ (الحديد: ٢٨)

Direct the believing men to restrain their eyes from looking at women outside the prohibited degrees so openly as to be sexually excited by them, and to cultivate the habit of guarding their looks. They should safeguard all their senses. For instance, they should not listen to the singing or beguiling voices of women outside the prohibited degrees nor should they listen to descriptions of their beauty. This is a good way of preserving the purity of their looks and hearts. In the same way, direct believing women that they should restrain their eyes from looking at men outside the prohibited degrees and should safeguard their ears against listening to the passionate voices of such men. They should cover up their beauty and should not disclose it to anyone outside the prohibited degrees. They should draw their head-coverings across their bosoms and should thus cover up their heads and ears and temples. They should not strike their feet on the ground like dancers. These are directions which can safeguard against moral stumbling (24:31-32).

The second method is to turn to God Almighty and to supplicate Him to be safeguarded against stumbling and slipping. Another direction is: Approach not adultery (17:33). This means that one should avoid all occasions that might incite one's mind in that direction, and should eschew all the paths that might lead to this vice. He who indulges in this vice carries his viciousness to the extreme. The way of adultery is an evil way as it obstructs one's progress towards the goal and is extremely harmful to the achievement of the purpose of life. Those who find no means of marriage should keep themselves chaste through the adoption of other means (24:34); for instance, through fasting or dieting or exercise.

People sometimes adopt celibacy or submit to castration and take up monasticism. God has not prescribed monasticism and that is why those who adopt it, prove unable to conform to its discipline (57:28). This is an indication that if celibacy and monasticism had been imposed by the Divine, everyone would have had to adopt this discipline, in which case the human race would have come to an end long ago. Also, if chastity had to be preserved through castration or any other such device, it would amount to criticism of the Divine Who has bestowed this capacity upon man. Besides, merit depends upon restraining the exercise of a capacity on an improper occasion, through fear of God, and thus acquiring double benefit through its proper exercise. By destroying the capacity a person would deprive himself of both benefits. Merit depends upon the possession of the capacity and its proper regulation. What merit would a person acquire who has lost that capacity and has become like a child? Does a child deserve merit because of his chastity?

Five Remedies Against Unchastity

In these verses God Almighty has not only set forth excellent teaching for acquiring the quality of chastity but has furnished man with five remedies against un-chastity. These are: to restrain one's eyes from gazing on those who are outside the prohibited degrees; to restrain one's ears from listening to their voices and to descriptions of their good looks; to avoid occasions which might furnish incitement towards this vice; and to control oneself during the period of celibacy through fasting, dieting etc.

We can confidently claim that this excellent teaching with all its devices that is set forth in the Holy Quran is peculiar to Islam. It should be kept in mind that as the natural condition of man, which is the source of his passions, is such that he cannot depart from it without a complete change in himself, his passions are bound to be roused, or in other words put in peril, when they are confronted with the occasion and opportunity for indulging in this vice. Therefore, God Almighty has not instructed us that we might freely gaze at women outside the prohibited degrees and might contemplate their beauty and observe all their movements in dancing etc. but that we should do so with pure looks. Nor have we been instructed to listen to the singing of these women and to lend ear to tales of their beauty, but that we should do so with a pure intent. We have been positively commanded not to look at their beauty, whether with pure intent or otherwise, nor to listen to their musical voices or to descriptions of their good looks, whether with pure intent or otherwise. We have been directed to eschew all this as we eschew carrion, so that we should not stumble. It is almost certain that our free glances would cause us to stumble sometime or the other. As God Almighty desires that our eyes and our hearts and all our limbs and organs should continue in a state of purity, He has furnished us with this excellent teaching. There can be no doubt that unrestrained looks become a source of danger. If we place soft bread before a hungry dog, it would be vain to hope that the dog should pay no attention to it. Thus God Almighty desired that human faculties should not be provided with any occasion for secret functioning and should not be confronted with anything that might incite dangerous tendencies.

This is the philosophy that underlies the Islamic regulations relating to the observance of the veil. The Book of God does not aim at keeping women in seclusion like prisoners. This is the concept of those who are not acquainted with the correct pattern of Islamic ways. The purpose of these regulations is to restrain men and women from letting their eyes to rove freely and from displaying their good looks and beauties, for therein lies the good both of men and of women. It should be remembered that to restrain one's looks and to direct them only towards observing that which is permissible is described in Arabic by the expression *ghadde basar*, which is the expression employed in the Holy Quran in this context. It does not behove a pious person who desires to keep his heart pure that he should lift his eyes freely in every direction like an animal. It is necessary that such a one should cultivate the habit of *ghadde basar* in his social life. This is a blessed habit through which his natural impulses would be converted into a high moral quality without interfering with his social needs. This is the quality which is called chastity in Islam.

The **second** quality in the context of the discarding of evil is the one known as honesty or integrity, that is to say, intolerance of the causing of harm to a fellow being by taking possession of his property dishonestly or unlawfully. Integrity is one of the natural conditions of man. That is why an infant, who follows his natural bent and who has not yet acquired any bad habit, so much dislikes anything belonging to another that it can only be persuaded with difficulty to be suckled by a wet nurse. If a wet nurse is not appointed for it while it is quite small and has not yet developed a keen consciousness. it becomes very difficult for a wet nurse to suckle it. It is naturally disinclined to be suckled by a woman other than its mother. This disinclination sometimes imposes great suffering upon it, and in extreme cases pushes it to the brink of death. What is the secret of this disinclination? It is that it naturally dislikes to leave its mother and to turn to something that belongs to another. When we reflect deeply upon this habit of an infant it becomes clear that this habit is at the root of all honesty and integrity. No one can be credited with the quality of integrity unless his heart becomes charged with dislike and hatred of the property of another as is the case with an infant. But an infant does not always employ this habit on its proper occasion and consequently imposes great suffering upon itself. This habit is only a natural condition which it exhibits involuntarily; it is not, therefore, a moral quality, though it is at the root of the moral quality of integrity. As an infant cannot be described as religious minded and trustworthy because of this habit, so also a person who does not exercise this natural habit on its proper occasion cannot be held to possess this moral quality. It is very difficult to become trustworthy and a person of integrity. Unless a person observes all aspects of integrity he cannot be judged truly trustworthy or honest. In this context God

Almighty has instructed us in different aspects of integrity in the following verses:

وَلَا تُؤْتُوا السُّفَهَآءَ اَمْوَالَكُمُ الَّتِيْ جَعَلَ اللهُ لَكُمْ قِيَمًا وَّارْزُقُوْهُمْ فِيْهَا وَاكْسُوْهُمْ وَقُوْلُوْا لَهُمْ قَوْلًا مَّعْرُوْفًا ۔

وَابْتَلُوا الْيَتٰمٰى حَتّٰى اِذَا بَلَغُوا النِّكَاحَ ۚ فَاِنْ اٰنَسْتُمْ مِّنْهُمْ رُشْدًا فَادْفَعُوْا اِلَيْهِمْ اَمْوَالَهُمْ ۚ وَلَا تَاْكُلُوْهَآ اِسْرَافًا وَّبِدَارًا اَنْ يَّكْبَرُوْا ۚ وَمَنْ كَانَ غَنِيًّا فَلْيَسْتَعْفِفْ ۚ وَمَنْ كَانَ فَقِيْرًا فَلْيَاْكُلْ بِالْمَعْرُوْفِ ۚ فَاِذَا دَفَعْتُمْ اِلَيْهِمْ اَمْوَالَهُمْ فَاَشْهِدُوْا عَلَيْهِمْ ۚ وَكَفٰى بِاللهِ حَسِيْبًا (النساء : ٦-٧)

وَلْيَخْشَ الَّذِيْنَ لَوْ تَرَكُوْا مِنْ خَلْفِهِمْ ذُرِّيَّةً ضِعٰفًا خَافُوْا عَلَيْهِمْ ۖ فَلْيَتَّقُوا اللهَ وَلْيَقُوْلُوْا قَوْلًا سَدِيْدًا ۚ اِنَّ الَّذِيْنَ يَاْكُلُوْنَ اَمْوَالَ الْيَتٰمٰى ظُلْمًا اِنَّمَا يَاْكُلُوْنَ فِيْ بُطُوْنِهِمْ نَارًا ۚ وَسَيَصْلَوْنَ سَعِيْرًا ۔ (النساء : ١٠-١١)

Should there be among you a person of property who is an orphan or minor and it is apprehended that he would waste his property through his lack of sense, you should take charge of his property as a custodian and should not hand it over to him, inasmuch as the whole system of commerce and social security depends upon proper care of property. Out of the income of the property you should provide for the maintenance of its owner and you should instruct him in all equitable values that would help to develop his reason and understanding and would furnish him with proper training so that he should not remain ignorant and inexperienced. If he is the son of a merchant he may be instructed in the ways of business and commerce, and if his father followed some profession or other occupation he may be given training in some appropriate occupation. Test him from time to time whether he is making progress in his training. When he arrives at the age of maturity, that is to say about 18 years, and you perceive that he has developed enough intelligence to look after his property, hand over his property to him. Do not deal with his property wastefully while it is in your charge, out of the apprehension that when he grows up he will take it over from you. If the custodian is in easy circumstances he should not make any charge for administering the property. But if he is poor, let him make use of as much of it as is fair.

The custom among Arab custodians of an orphan's property was that the property was used as capital for commerce and out of its profit provision was made for the orphan and thus the capital was not destroyed. The custodian made a fair charge for looking after the property. This is the system to which reference is made in these verses. Then it is said: When you hand over the property to its owner you should do so before witnesses (4:6-7).

Those of you who are likely to leave behind minor children should give no directions by way of testament which should operate unfairly against the children. Those who consume the substance of orphans unjustly only devour fire into their bellies and shall enter a blazing fire (4:10-11).

It is to be observed how many aspects of honesty and integrity God Almighty has set forth in these verses. A truly honest person is one who keeps in mind all these aspects. If this is not done with perfect intelligence his trustworthiness would cover many hidden dishonesties.

Then it is directed:

وَ لَا تَأْكُلُوٓا أَمْوَالَكُمْ بَيْنَكُمْ بِالْبَاطِلِ وَتُدْلُوْا بِهَآ
اِلَى الْحُكَّامِ لِتَأْكُلُوْا فَرِيْقًا مِّنْ اَمْوَالِ النَّاسِ بِالْاِثْمِ
وَ اَنْتُمْ تَعْلَمُوْنَ (البقرة : ١٨٩)

اِنَّ اللّٰهَ يَأْمُرُكُمْ اَنْ تُؤَدُّوا الْاَمٰنٰتِ اِلٰٓى اَهْلِهَا ـ (النِّسَاء: ٥٩)

اِنَّ اللّٰهَ لَا يُحِبُّ الْخَآئِنِيْنَ ـ (الانفال : ٥٩)

وَاَوْفُوا الْكَيْلَ اِذَا كِلْتُمْ وَزِنُوْا بِالْقِسْطَاسِ الْمُسْتَقِيْمِ ـ (بنى اسرائيل ٣٦)

وَ لَا تَبْخَسُوا النَّاسَ اَشْيَآءَهُمْ وَلَا تَعْثَوْا فِى الْاَرْضِ

مُفْسِدِيْنَ ـ (الشعراء: ١٨٤)

وَ لَا تَتَبَدَّلُوا الْخَبِيْثَ بِالطَّيِّبِ ـ (النِّسَاء : ٣)

Do not devour each other's substance through deceit and falsehood, nor offer your wealth as a bribe to the authorities, that you may deliberately acquire a part of other people's wealth through injustice (2:189). Make over the trusts to those entitled to them (4:59). Allah does not love those who are dishonest (8:59). Give full measure when you measure out, and weigh out with a true balance (17:36). Do not deliver short, and do not go about creating disorder in the land (26:184). This means that you should not go about in the land with an evil intent, to commit theft or robbery or to pick pockets or to acquire the property of other people through unlawful means. Do not give that which is defective in exchange for that which is good (4:3); that is to say, as embezzlement is unlawful, so the sale of defective articles representing them as being in good condition, and the exchange of defective articles in return for good ones, is also unlawful.

In all these verses God Almighty has set forth all dishonest practices in such a comprehensive way that no type of dishonesty has been omitted. He has not merely forbidden theft, lest a stupid person should consider that though theft is forbidden all other improper methods of acquiring property are permitted. Forbidding all improper methods of acquiring property in a comprehensive way is true wisdom. In short, if a person does not possess the quality of integrity in all its aspects, he would not be considered honest even if he exhibits honesty in certain matters. That would be only his natural condition, shorn of reasonable discrimination and true insight.

The *third* moral quality in the context of discarding evil is designated in Arabic as *hudnah* or *haun*, which means refraining from inflicting physical pain on anyone and behaving peacefully. Without a doubt, peacefulness is a high moral quality and is essential for humanity. The natural impulse corresponding to this moral quality, the regulation of which converts it into a moral quality, which is possessed by an infant, is attachment. It is obvious that in his natural condition man is unable to conceive of peacefulness or combativeness. In that condition the impulse of attachment that he exhibits is the root of peacefulness, but as it is not exercised under the control of reason or reflection and with deliberation, it is not accounted a moral quality. It becomes a moral quality when a person deliberately makes himself harmless and exercises the quality of peacefulness on its proper occasion, and refrains from using it out of place. In this context the Divine teaching is:

$$وَاَصْلِحُوْا ذَاتَ بَيْنِكُمْ ۔ (الانفال : ٢)$$

$$وَالصُّلْحُ خَيْرٌ ط ۔ (النِّسَاء : ١٢٩)$$

وَإِنْ جَنَحُوا لِلسَّلْمِ فَاجْنَحْ لَهَا (الانفال : ٦٢)

عِبَادُ الرَّحْمٰنِ الَّذِيْنَ يَمْشُوْنَ عَلَى الْأَرْضِ هَوْنًا (الفرقان:٦٤)

وَإِذَا مَرُّوا بِاللَّغْوِ مَرُّوا كِرَامًا (الفرقان : ٧٣)

اِدْفَعْ بِالَّتِيْ هِيَ اَحْسَنُ فَاِذَا الَّذِيْ بَيْنَكَ وَ بَيْنَهٗ عَدَاوَةٌ كَاَنَّهٗ وَلِيٌّ حَمِيْمٌ (حٰمٓ السجدة : ٣٥)

Try to promote accord between yourselves (8:2); Peace is best (4:129); when they incline towards peace, do you incline towards it also (8:62). The true servants of the Gracious One walk upon the earth in humility (25:64); and when they come upon something vain, which might develop into strife, they pass on with dignity (25:73), that is to say, they do not start quarrelling over trifles and do not make small matters which do not cause much harm an occasion for discord. The expression "vain" that is employed in this verse means mischievous utterance of words or doing something which causes little damage and does little harm. Peacefulness means that one should overlook conduct of that type and should act with dignity; but if a person's conduct does real harm to life or property or honour, the moral quality that should come into play in apposition to it is not peacefulness but forbearance, to which we shall revert later. Should anyone behave mischievously towards you, you should try to repel it with peacefulness, whereby he who is your enemy will become your warm friend (41:35). In short, peacefulness means overlooking trivial matters of annoyance which occasion no great harm, and are more or less confined to uttering nonsense.

The *fourth* moral quality in the context of discarding evil is courtesy or a good word. The natural impulse which is at the root of this moral quality is cheerfulness. Before an infant is able to express itself in words, it displays cheerfulness as a substitute for courtesy and good talk. That shows that the root of courtesy is cheerfulness which is a natural faculty and is converted into the moral quality of courtesy by being used on its proper occasion. The Divine teaching in this context is:

وَقُوْلُوْا لِلنَّاسِ حُسْنًا۔ (البقرة: ٨٤)

لَا يَسْخَرْ قَوْمٌ مِّنْ قَوْمٍ عَسَى اَنْ يَّكُوْنُوْا خَيْرًا مِّنْهُمْ وَلَا نِسَاۤءٌ مِّنْ نِّسَاۤءٍ عَسَى اَنْ يَّكُنَّ خَيْرًا مِّنْهُنَّ وَلَا تَلْمِزُوْا اَنْفُسَكُمْ وَلَا تَنَابَزُوْا بِالْاَلْقَابِ (الحجرات: ١١)

اِجْتَنِبُوْا كَثِيْرًا مِّنَ الظَّنِّ اِنَّ بَعْضَ الظَّنِّ اِثْمٌ وَّلَا تَجَسَّسُوْا وَلَا يَغْتَبْ بَعْضُكُمْ بَعْضًا... وَاتَّقُوا اللّٰهَ اِنَّ اللّٰهَ تَوَّابٌ رَّحِيْمٌ (الحجرات: ١٢)

وَلَا تَقْفُ مَا لَيْسَ لَكَ بِهٖ عِلْمٌ اِنَّ السَّمْعَ وَالْبَصَرَ وَالْفُؤَادَ كُلُّ اُولٰٓئِكَ كَانَ عَنْهُ مَسْـُٔوْلًا (بنی اسرائیل: ٣٧)

Say to people that which is good (2:84). Let not one people deride another people, haply they may be better than themselves; nor let one group of women deride another, haply the last may be better than the first. Defame not your people nor call them names (49:12). Eschew too much suspicion; Also spy not, nor backbite one another (49:13). Do not charge anyone with anything of which you have no proof, and remember that the ear and the eye and the heart will all be called to account (17:37).

Moral Qualities Related to the Doing of Good

The second type of moral qualities are those that are related to doing good. The first of these is forbearance or forgiveness. He who commits an offence against another causes him pain or harm and deserves to be punished either through the process of the law, with imprisonment or fine, or directly by the person offended. To forgive him, if forgiveness should be appropriate, would be to do him good. In this context the teaching of the Holy Quran is:

وَ الْكَاظِمِيْنَ الْغَيْظَ وَ الْعَافِيْنَ عَنِ النَّاسِ ـ رال عمران: ١٣٥،

جَزٰٓؤُا سَيِّئَةٍ سَيِّئَةٌ مِّثْلُهَا ۚ فَمَنْ عَفَا وَاَصْلَحَ فَاَجْرُهٗ

عَلَى اللّٰهِ ـ رالشورٰی: ٤١،

Those who control their tempers when they are roused and who overlook people's faults when that is appropriate (3:135). The recompense of an injury is a penalty in proportion thereto; but whoso forgives and effects thereby a reform in the offender, and no harm is apprehended, that is to say, exercises forgiveness on its appropriate occasion, will have his reward with Allah (42:41).

This verse shows that the Quran does not teach non-resistance to evil on all occasions, or that mischief makers and wrongdoers should never be punished. Its teaching is that one must consider whether the occasion calls for forgiveness or punishment, and to adopt the course which would be best in the interests both of the offender and the public. Sometimes an offender turns away from wrongdoing in consequence of being forgiven, and sometimes forgiveness incites him to further wrongdoing. Therefore, God Almighty directs that we should not develop the habit of forgiving blindly on all occasions, but should consider carefully whether forgiveness or punishment would be most appropriate, and, therefore, a virtue, in each particular case, and should adopt that course. Some people are so vindictive that they keep in mind the wrongs done to their fathers through generations, and there are others who carry forbearance and forgiveness to the extreme, sometimes even to the limit of shamelessness. They exercise such weakness, forgiveness and forbearance as are utterly inconsistent with dignity, honour, and chastity. Their conduct is a stain on good character and the result of their forgiveness and forbearance is that people are disgusted with them. That is why the Holy Quran attaches the condition of appropriate time and place for the exercise of every moral quality, and does not approve the exercise of a moral quality out of its place.

It should be remembered that forgiveness is not a moral quality in itself. It is a natural impulse which is found in children also. A child soon forgets an injury, if it is inflicted upon him wrongfully, and again approaches affectionately the person who has inflicted the injury upon him, even if such a person should intend to kill him. He is pleased with his beguiling words. Such forgiveness is in no sense a moral quality. It would become a moral quality when it is exercised in its proper place and on its proper occasion; otherwise it would only be a natural impulse. There are few people who are able to distinguish between a natural impulse and a moral quality. We have repeatedly pointed out the distinction between a true moral quality and a natural condition, which is that a moral quality is conditioned by conformity to place and occasion, and a natural impulse often comes into play out of place. A cow is harmless and a goat is humble but we do not attribute these qualities to them because they are not invested with a sense of time and place. Divine wisdom and God's true and perfect Book have made every moral quality subject to time and place for its proper exercise.

The second moral quality in this category is equity, and the third is benevolence and the fourth is graciousness as between kindred. God, the Glorious, has said:

$$اِنَّ اللهَ يَأْمُرُ بِالْعَدْلِ وَالْاِحْسَانِ وَاِيْتَآئِ ذِى الْقُرْبٰى وَيَنْهٰى عَنِ الْفَحْشَآءِ وَالْمُنْكَرِ وَالْبَغْىِ$$

(النحـل: ٩١)

This means that we are commanded to return good for good, and to exercise benevolence when it is called for, and to do good with natural eagerness as between kindred, when that should be appropriate (16:91). God Almighty forbids transgression or that you should exercise benevolence out of place or should refrain from exercising it when it is called for; or that you should fall short of exercising graciousness as between kindred on its proper occasion, or should extend it beyond its appropriate limit. This verse sets forth three gradations of doing good.

The *first* is the doing of good in return for good. This is the lowest gradation and even an average person can easily acquire this gradation that he should do good to those who do good to him.

The *second* gradation is a little more difficult than the first, and that is to take the initiative in doing good out of pure benevolence. This is the middle grade. Most people act benevolently towards the poor, but there is a hidden deficiency in benevolence, that the person exercising benevolence is conscious of it and desires gratitude or prayer in return for his benevolence. If on any occasion the other person should turn against him, he considers him ungrateful. On occasion he reminds him of his benevolence or puts some heavy burden upon him. The benevolent ones have been admonished by God Almighty:

لَا تُبْطِلُوا صَدَقْتِكُمْ بِالْمَنِّ وَالْأَذَىٰ - رَالبِقَرَة: ٢٦٥)

Render not vain your alms by reproaches or injury (2:265).
The Arabic word for alms (*Sadaqah*) is derived from a root
(*sidq*) that means sincerity. If the heart is not inspired by sincerity
in bestowing alms, the almsgiving ceases to be alms and becomes
mere display. That is why those who exercise benevolence have
been admonished by God Almighty not to render vain their
benevolence by reproaches or injury.

The third grade of doing good is graciousness as between
kindred. God Almighty directs that in this grade there should be
no idea of benevolence or any desire for gratitude, but good
should be done out of such eager sympathy as, for instance, a
mother does good to her child. This is the highest grade of doing
good which cannot be exceeded. But God Almighty has
conditioned all these grades of doing good with their appropriate
time and place. The verse cited above clearly indicates that if
these virtues are not exercised in their proper places they would
become vices. For instance, if equity exceeds its limits it would
take on an unwholesome aspect and would become indecent. In
the same way, misuse of benevolence would take on a form
which would be repelled by reason and conscience; and in the
same way graciousness between kindred would become
transgression. The Arabic word for transgression is *baghy*, which
connotes excessive rain which ruins crops. A deficiency in the
discharge of an obligation or an excess in its discharge are both
baghy. In short, whichever of these three qualities is exercised
out of place becomes tainted. That is why they are all three
qualities conditioned by the due observance of place and
occasion. It should be remembered that equity or benevolence or
graciousness between kindred are not in themselves moral
qualities. They are man's natural conditions and faculties that are
exhibited even by children before they develop their reason.

Reason is a condition of the exercise of a moral quality and there
is also a condition that every moral quality should be exercised in
its proper place and on its proper occasion.

There are several other directions set out in the Holy Quran
concerning benevolence which are all made subject to the
condition of place and time.

It is said:

يَاۤاَيُّهَا الَّذِيْنَ اٰمَنُوۤا اَنْفِقُوْا مِنْ طَيِّبٰتِ مَا كَسَبْتُمْ

وَلَا تَيَمَّمُوا الْخَبِيْثَ مِنْهُ ـ (البقرة : ٢٦٨)

لَا تُبْطِلُوْا صَدَقٰتِكُمْ بِالْمَنِّ وَ الْاَذٰى كَالَّذِىْ يُنْفِقُ

مَالَهٗ رِئَاۤءَ النَّاسِ ـ (البقرة : ٢٦٥)

اَحْسِنُوْا اِنَّ اللّٰهَ يُحِبُّ الْمُحْسِنِيْنَ ـ (البقرة : ١٩٧)

اِنَّ الْاَبْرَارَ يَشْرَبُوْنَ مِنْ كَاْسٍ كَانَ مِزَاجُهَا كَافُوْرًا ـ

عَيْنًا يَّشْرَبُ بِهَا عِبَادُ اللّٰهِ يُفَجِّرُوْنَهَا تَفْجِيْرًا ـ .....

وَيُطْعِمُوْنَ الطَّعَامَ عَلٰى حُبِّهٖ مِسْكِيْنًا وَّ يَتِيْمًا

وَّ اَسِيْرًا اِنَّمَا نُطْعِمُكُمْ لِوَجْهِ اللّٰهِ لَا نُرِيْدُ مِنْكُمْ

جَزَاۤءً وَّلَا شُكُوْرًا ـ (الدهر : ٧ ـ ١٠)

وَاٰتَى الْمَالَ عَلٰى حُبِّهٖ ذَوِى الْقُرْبٰى وَ الْيَتٰمٰى وَ الْمَسٰكِيْنَ

وَابْنَ السَّبِيْلِ وَ السَّآئِلِيْنَ وَ فِى الرِّقَابِ (البقرة : ١٧٨)

وَالَّذِيْنَ اِذَاۤ اَنْفَقُوْا لَمْ يُسْرِفُوْا وَ لَمْ يَقْتُرُوْا وَكَانَ

بَيْنَ ذٰلِكَ قَوَامًا (الفرقان : ٦٨)

وَالَّذِيْنَ يَصِلُوْنَ مَآ أَمَرَ اللّٰهُ بِهٖ أَنْ يُّوْصَلَ وَ
يَخْشَوْنَ رَبَّهُمْ وَيَخَافُوْنَ سُوْءَ الْحِسَابِ (الرعد:۲۲)

وَفِيْٓ أَمْوَالِهِمْ حَقٌّ لِّلسَّآئِلِ وَالْمَحْرُوْمِ (الذاريات:۲۰)

الَّذِيْنَ يُنْفِقُوْنَ فِى السَّرَّآءِ وَالضَّرَّآءِ ـ (رأل عمران:۱۳۵)

وَأَنْفَقُوْا مِمَّا رَزَقْنٰهُمْ سِرًّا وَّعَلَانِيَةً (الرعد:۲۳)

اِنَّمَا الصَّدَقٰتُ لِلْفُقَرَآءِ وَالْمَسٰكِيْنِ وَالْعٰمِلِيْنَ
عَلَيْهَا وَالْمُؤَلَّفَةِ قُلُوْبُهُمْ وَفِى الرِّقَابِ وَالْغٰرِمِيْنَ
وَفِيْ سَبِيْلِ اللّٰهِ وَابْنِ السَّبِيْلِ فَرِيْضَةً مِّنَ اللّٰهِ
وَاللّٰهُ عَلِيْمٌ حَكِيْمٌ ـ (التوبة:۶۰)

لَنْ تَنَالُوا الْبِرَّ حَتّٰى تُنْفِقُوْا مِمَّا تُحِبُّوْنَ ـ (رأل عمران:۹۳)

وَآتِ ذَا الْقُرْبٰى حَقَّهٗ وَالْمِسْكِيْنَ وَابْنَ السَّبِيْلِ
وَلَا تُبَذِّرْ تَبْذِيْرًا ـ (بنى اسرآءيل:۲۷)

بِالْوَالِدَيْنِ اِحْسَانًا وَّبِذِى الْقُرْبٰى وَالْيَتٰمٰى وَالْمَسٰكِيْنِ
وَالْجَارِ ذِى الْقُرْبٰى وَالْجَارِ الْجُنُبِ وَالصَّاحِبِ بِالْجَنْبِ
وَابْنِ السَّبِيْلِ وَمَا مَلَكَتْ أَيْمَانُكُمْ اِنَّ اللّٰهَ لَا يُحِبُّ مَنْ
كَانَ مُخْتَالًا فَخُوْرَا اِلَّذِيْنَ يَبْخَلُوْنَ وَ يَأْمُرُوْنَ
النَّاسَ بِالْبُخْلِ وَيَكْتُمُوْنَ مَآ اٰتٰهُمُ اللّٰهُ مِنْ فَضْلِهٖ ـ
(النِّسَآء:۳۷-۳۸)

O ye who believe, spend by way of generosity or benevolence or charity such of your wealth as you have acquired lawfully, that is to say, no part of which has been acquired through theft or bribery or dishonesty or embezzlement or wrongdoing. Do not select for charity out of it that which is useless or unclean (2:268).

Render not vain your alms with reproaches or injury, that is to say, never remind your donee that you had bestowed anything on him nor inflict any injury upon him, for in such case your charity would be rendered vain, nor spend your money merely for display (2:265). Be benevolent towards your fellow beings, for Allah loves those who are benevolent (2:196).

The truly virtuous shall drink of a cup tempered with camphor (76:6-7). The reference to camphor means that their hearts will be cleansed of all the burning desires and impure urges of the world. The root of the Arabic word for camphor connotes suppression, or covering up, which means that their illicit emotions will be suppressed and they will become pure hearted and will enjoy the coolness of understanding. Then it is said that they will drink from a spring which they shall cause to gush forth from the earth through their efforts (76:8). This indicates a deep mystery of the philosophy of paradise. Let him who has understanding understand it.

The truly virtuous feed the poor, the orphan, and the captive for the love of Allah with such foods as they eat themselves, assuring them: We are not laying you under any obligation but feed you only to win Allah's pleasure. We desire no return or thanks from you (76:9-10). This is an indication that they exercise the third grade of doing good which proceeds out of pure sympathy.

The truly virtuous are in the habit of spending their wealth out of love of God on their kindred and on the upbringing and training of orphans and in making provision for the poor and for providing comfort for travellers and for those who ask and for procuring the freedom of slaves and discharging the burdens of those who are in debt (2:178).

They are neither extravagant nor niggardly, but keep a balance between the two (25:68). They join together that which Allah has bidden to be joined, and fear their Lord (13:22). In their wealth those who ask and those who are unable to ask have a right (51:20). By those who are unable to ask are meant animals such as dogs, cats, sparrows, oxen, donkeys, goats and others that cannot express their needs in words.

They do not hold back in times of scarcity or famine, but continue to spend at such times also according to their capacity (3:135). They spend in charity secretly and openly (13:23); secretly, so that they might safeguard themselves against displaying their charity, and openly, so that they might set an example for others. That which is set aside for charity should be spent on the poor and the needy, and on those employed in connection with its collection and distribution, and to help those who have to be rescued from some evil, and on procuring the freedom of slaves, and on those burdened with debts, and the afflicted and on other purposes which are purely for the sake of God and on those striving in the cause of Allah (9:60).

You cannot attain the highest grade of virtue unless you spend for the promotion of the welfare of your fellow beings that part of your wealth which you hold dear (3:93).

Render to the poor their due and to the needy and the wayfarer but safeguard yourselves against extravagance (17:27). This is a direction to restrain people from spending unnecessarily on weddings and luxuries and on the occasion of the birth of a child etc.

Be benevolent towards parents and kindred, and orphans and the needy and the neighbour who is a kinsman, and the neighbour who is not related to you, and the wayfarer and your servants and your horses and your cattle and your other animals that you possess. This is what God loves. He loves not those who are heedless and selfish, and those who are niggardly and enjoin other people to be niggardly, and conceal their wealth and tell those who are needy that they have nothing which they can give them (4:37-38).

True Courage

Of the natural conditions of man is that which resembles courage, as an infant sometimes seeks to thrust his hand into the fire on account of its natural condition of fearlessness. In that condition a person fearlessly confronts tigers and other wild beasts and issues forth alone to fight a large number of people. Such a one is considered very brave. But this is only a natural condition that is found even in savage animals and in dogs. True courage which is one of the high moral qualities is conditioned by place and occasion, which are mentioned in the Holy Word of God as follows:

وَالصّٰبِرِيْنَ فِى الْبَاْسَآءِ وَالضّرَّآءِ وَحِيْنَ الْبَاْسِ ﴿البقرة: ١٧٨﴾

وَالَّذِيْنَ صَبَرُوا ابْتِغَآءَ وَجْهِ رَبِّهِمْ ـ ﴿الرعد: ٢٣﴾

اَلَّذِيْنَ قَالَ لَهُمُ النَّاسُ اِنَّ النَّاسَ قَدْ جَمَعُوْا لَكُمْ

فَاخْشَوْهُمْ فَزَادَهُمْ اِيْمَانًا ۖ وَّقَالُوا حَسْبُنَا اللّٰهُ

وَ نِعْمَ الْوَكِيْلُ ـ ﴿ال عمران: ١٧٤﴾

وَلَا تَكُوْنُوْا كَالَّذِيْنَ خَرَجُوْا مِنْ دِيَارِهِمْ بَطَرًا وَّ

رِئَآءَ النَّاسِ ﴿الانفال: ٤٨﴾

Those who are steadfast in adversity and under affliction and in battle (2:178); their steadfastness is for the purpose of seeking the countenance of Allah and not for the display of bravery (13:23). They are threatened that people have gathered together to persecute them and they should be afraid of them, but this only adds to their faith and they say: Sufficient for us is Allah (3:174). Thus their courage and bravery are not like that of dogs and wild animals which proceed from natural passions and are only one-sided. Their courage has two aspects. Sometimes they contend out of their personal courage against the passions of their selves and overcome them; and sometimes when they feel that it is appropriate to fight against an enemy they issue forth against him, not out of any urge of a roused self but for the support of truth. They do not depend upon their selves but trust in God and behave courageously. They do not issue forth from their homes insolently and to be seen of people. Their only purpose is to win the pleasure of God (8:48).

These verses illustrate that true courage derives from steadfastness. To be steadfast against every personal passion or against any calamity that attacks like an enemy and not to run away out of cowardice is true courage. Thus, there is a great difference between human courage and the courage of a wild beast. A wild animal is moved only in one direction when it is roused, but a man who possesses true courage chooses confrontation or non-resistance whichever might be appropriate to the occasion.

Truthfulness

One of the natural qualities of man is truthfulness. Normally, unless a person is moved by some selfish motive, he does not wish to tell a lie. He is averse to falsehood and is reluctant to have recourse to it. He is displeased with a person who is proved to have told a lie, and looks down upon him. But this natural

inclination cannot be accounted a moral quality. Even children
and the insane exhibit it. Unless a person discards those purposes
which lead him away from telling the truth, he cannot be
considered truthful. If a person tells the truth where no personal
interest is involved, but is ready to have recourse to a falsehood
where his honour or property or life is concerned, and fails to tell
the truth, is no better than a child or an insane person. Do not the
insane and minors speak such truth? There is scarcely anyone in
the world who would tell a lie without any purpose. The truth
that might be abandoned in order to escape some loss that
threatens is not a moral quality. The proper occasion of telling
the truth is when one apprehends loss of life or property or
honour. In this context Divine teaching is:

فَاجْتَنِبُوا الرِّجْسَ مِنَ الْاَوْثَانِ وَاجْتَنِبُوا قَوْلَ

الزُّوْرِ ﴿الحج: ٣١﴾

وَلَا يَأْبَ الشُّهَدَآءُ اِذَا مَا دُعُوْا ﴿البقرة: ٢٨٣﴾

وَلَا تَكْتُمُوا الشَّهَادَةَ وَمَنْ يَّكْتُمْهَا فَاِنَّهٗ اٰثِمٌ قَلْبُهٗ ﴿البقرة: ٢٨٤﴾

وَاِذَا قُلْتُمْ فَاعْدِلُوْا وَلَوْ كَانَ ذَا قُرْبٰى ﴿الانعام: ١٥٣﴾

كُوْنُوْا قَوّٰمِيْنَ بِالْقِسْطِ شُهَدَآءَ لِلّٰهِ وَلَوْ عَلٰى اَنْفُسِكُمْ

اَوِ الْوَالِدَيْنِ وَالْاَقْرَبِيْنَ ﴿النساء: ١٣٧﴾

وَلَا يَجْرِمَنَّكُمْ شَنَاٰنُ قَوْمٍ عَلٰى اَلَّا تَعْدِلُوْا ﴿المائدة: ٩﴾

وَالصّٰدِقِيْنَ وَالصّٰدِقٰتِ ﴿الاحزاب: ٣٦﴾

وَ تَوَاصَوْا بِالْحَقِّ ه وَ تَوَاصَوْا بِالصَّبْرِ ـ رالعصر: ٤ ›

لَا يَشْهَدُوْنَ الزُّوْرَ ـ ر الفرقان: ٧٣ ›

Shun the abomination of idols, and shun all words of falsehood (22:31). This shows that falsehood is also an idol and he who relies upon it ceases to trust in God. Thus, by uttering a lie one loses God.

When you are called upon to testify to the truth, do not fail to do so (2:283); and do not conceal true testimony, and he who conceals it has a sinful heart (2:284).

When you speak, tell the truth and hold the scales even, though the person concerned be your kinsman (6:153).

Be strict in observing justice and bear witness only for the sake of Allah, even if it should occasion loss to you or your parents or your kinsmen or sons, etc. (4:136). Let not the enmity of a people towards you incite you to injustice or falsehood (5:9). Truthful men and truthful women will have a great reward from Allah (33:36). They exhort one another to hold fast to the truth (103:4). Those who do not keep company with the untruthful (25:73).

Steadfastness

One of the natural qualities of man is steadfastness during illness and under afflictions. He has recourse to patience after much complaining and sorrowing. It is natural that a person cries and groans under affliction and in the end, after giving vent to his grievance, he beats a retreat. Both these conditions are natural but are not in any sense part of a moral quality. In this context the relevant moral quality is that when one suffers a loss, one should consider it as rendering back to God that which He had bestowed, and should utter no complaint about it. One should affirm that it was a bounty of God which He has recalled and that

one is reconciled to God's pleasure. In this context the Holy
Quran admonishes us:

$$
\text{وَ لَنَبْلُوَنَّكُمْ بِشَىْءٍ مِّنَ الْخَوْفِ وَالْجُوْعِ وَنَقْصٍ مِّنَ}
$$

$$
\text{الْاَمْوَالِ وَالْاَنْفُسِ وَالثَّمَرَاتِ وَبَشِّرِ الصّٰبِرِيْنَ}
$$

$$
\text{الَّذِيْنَ اِذَآ اَصَابَتْهُمْ مُّصِيْبَةٌ قَالُوْآ اِنَّا لِلّٰهِ وَاِنَّآ}
$$

$$
\text{اِلَيْهِ رٰجِعُوْنَ - اُولٰٓئِكَ عَلَيْهِمْ صَلَوٰتٌ مِّنْ رَّبِّهِمْ}
$$

$$
\text{وَرَحْمَةٌ ۖ وَ اُولٰٓئِكَ هُمُ الْمُهْتَدُوْنَ -}
$$

(البقرة : ١٥٤-١٥٨)

We shall surely try you with somewhat of fear, and hunger,
and loss of wealth, and lives, and of the fruits of your labour and
sometimes your dear children will die; then give glad tidings to
the steadfast, who, when a misfortune overtakes them, do not
lose heart, but affirm: We belong to God and are His servants and
to Him shall we return. It is these on whom are blessings from
their Lord and mercy, and it is these who are rightly guided
(2:156-157).

This moral quality is called steadfastness or reconciliation to
the Divine will. From one aspect it might be called equity or
justice. Throughout a person's life, God Almighty manifests
thousands of matters in accord with the wishes of a person and
bestows numberless bounties upon him, so that it would be
inequitable on his part that on such occasions when God calls
upon him to submit to His will, he should turn away, not pleased
with the will of God, and should be critical, or lose faith or go
astray.

Sympathy for Mankind

Of the natural qualities of man is his sympathy for his fellow beings. The followers of every religion have natural sympathy for their own people and many of them, under the urge of such sympathy, act wrongfully towards other people, as if they do not regard them as human beings. This state cannot be described as a moral quality. It is a natural urge which is manifested even by birds. For instance, when one crow dies hundreds of crows flock together. This quality would be accounted a high moral quality when it is exercised on its proper occasion justly and equitably. It would be a great moral quality which is designated sympathy both in Arabic and Persian. This is referred to by Allah, the Exalted in the Holy Quran. God Almighty has directed in the Holy Quran:

وَتَعَاوَنُوْا عَلَى الْبِرِّ وَالتَّقْوٰى وَلَا تَعَاوَنُوْا عَلَى الْاِثْمِ وَالْعُدْوَانِ ـ (المائدة : ٣)

وَلَا تَهِنُوْا فِى ابْتِغَآءِ الْقَوْمِ ـ (النساء: ١٠٥)

وَلَا تَكُنْ لِّلْخَآئِنِيْنَ خَصِيْمًا ـ (النساء: ١٠٦)

وَلَا تُجَادِلْ عَنِ الَّذِيْنَ يَخْتَانُوْنَ اَنْفُسَهُمْ اِنَّ اللّٰهَ لَا يُحِبُّ مَنْ كَانَ خَوَّانًا اَثِيْمًا ـ (النساء: ١٠٨)

Assist one another in piety and rectitude, and assist not one another in sin and transgression (5:3).

Slacken not in serving your fellow beings (4:105). Contend not on behalf of the treacherous (4:106). Plead not on behalf of those who persist in being unfaithful. Allah loves not those who are perfidious (4:108)[1].

Search for an Exalted Being

Of the natural conditions of man is his search after an Exalted Being towards Whom he has an inherent attraction. This is manifested by an infant from the moment of its birth. As soon as it is born, it displays a spiritual characteristic that it inclines towards its mother and is inspired by love of her. As its faculties are developed and its nature begins to display itself openly, this inherent quality is displayed more and more strongly. It finds no comfort anywhere except in the lap of its mother. If it is separated from her and finds itself at a distance from her, its life becomes bitter. Heaps of bounties fail to beguile it away from its mother in whom all its joy is concentrated. It feels no joy apart from her. What, then, is the nature of the attraction which an infant feels so strongly towards its mother?

It is the attraction which the True Creator has implanted in the nature of man. The same attraction comes into play whenever a person feels love for another. It is a reflection of the attraction that is inherent in man's nature towards God, as if he is in search of something that he misses, the name of which he has forgotten and which he seeks to find in one thing or another which he takes up from time to time. A person's love of wealth or offspring or wife or his soul being attracted towards a musical voice are all

---

1. Here Hudhur mentions two categories of verses. In the first category are those verses which deal with compassion for God's creation and with the idea of collaboration in the doing of good deeds. In the second category, the subject of discussion is the punishment of the wrongdoer when the situation so demands. The message being conveyed is that sympathy for humankind does not mean that the culprit merely be punished for his wrongdoings thus securing the rest of society from his transgressions. In fact punishing him is an aspect of sympathy for humankind. (The Publishers)

indications of his search for the True Beloved. As man cannot behold with his physical eyes the Imperceptible Being, Who is latent like the quality of fire in everyone, but is hidden, nor can he discover Him through the mere exercise of imperfect reason, he has been misled grievously in his search and has mistakenly assigned His position to others. The Holy Quran has, in this context, set forth an excellent illustration, to the effect that the world is like a palace, the floor of which is paved with smooth slabs of glass, under which flows a rapid current of water. Every eye that beholds this floor mistakenly imagines it to be running water. A person fears to tread upon the floor as he would be afraid of treading upon running water, though in reality the floor is only paved with smooth transparent slabs of glass. Thus these heavenly bodies like the sun and the moon etc. are the smooth and transparent slabs of glass under which a great power is in operation like a fast flowing current of water. It is a great mistake on the part of those who worship these heavenly bodies that they attribute to them that which is manifested by the power that operates behind them. This is the interpretation of the verse of the Holy Quran:

إِنَّهُ صَرْحٌ مُّمَرَّدٌ مِّن قَوَارِيرَ - رالنمل : ٤٥،

It is a great hall paved with smooth slabs of glass (27:45).

In short, as the Being of God Almighty, despite its brilliance, is utterly hidden, this physical system that is spread out before our eyes is not alone sufficient for its recognition. That is why those who have depended upon this system and have observed carefully its perfect and complete orderliness together with all the wonders comprehended in it, and have thoroughly studied astronomy, physics, and philosophy, and have, as it were, penetrated into the heavens and the earth, have yet not been delivered from the darkness of doubts and suspicions. Many of them become involved in grave errors and wander far away in pursuit of their stupid fancies. Their utmost conjecture is that this grand system which displays great wisdom must have a Maker, but this conjecture is incomplete and this insight is defective. The affirmation that this system must have a creator does not amount to a positive affirmation that He does in truth exist. Such a conjecture cannot bestow satisfaction upon the heart, nor remove all doubt from it. Nor is it a draught which can quench the thirst for complete understanding which man's nature demands. Indeed, this defective understanding is most dangerous, for despite all its noise it amounts to nothing.

In short, unless God Almighty affirms His existence through His Word, as He has manifested it through His work, the observation of the work alone does not afford complete satisfaction[2]. For instance, if we are confronted by a room the door of which is bolted from inside, our immediate reaction would be that there is someone inside the room who has bolted the door from inside, inasmuch as it is apparently impossible to bolt a door from inside by some device employed for the purpose from the outside. But if, despite persistent calls from the outside over a period of years, no response becomes audible from inside, our supposition that there must be someone inside would have to be abandoned and we would be compelled to conclude that the door has been bolted from inside through some clever device. This is the situation in which those philosophers have placed themselves whose understanding is limited solely to the observation of the work of God. It is a great mistake to imagine that God is like a corpse interred in the earth whose recovery is the business of man. If God has only been discovered through human effort, it is vain to expect anything from Him. Indeed, God has, through eternity, called mankind to Himself by

2. This means that without the Word of God, contemplation of and foresight into the laws of nature cannot be sufficient. (The Publishers)

affirming: I am present. It would be a great impertinence to imagine that man has laid God under an obligation by discovering Him through his own effort, and that if there had been no philosophers He would have continued unknown.

It is equally stupid to enquire how can God speak unless He has a tongue to speak with? The answer is: Has He not created the earth and the heavenly bodies without physical hands? Does He not view the universe without eyes? Does He not hear our supplications without physical ears?

Then is it not necessary that He should also speak to us? Nor is it correct to say that God spoke in the past but does not speak now. We cannot limit His Word or His discourse to any particular time. He is as ready today to enrich His seekers from the fountain of revelation as He was at any time, and the gates of His grace are as wide open today as they were at any time. It is true, however, that as the need for a perfect law has been fulfilled all law and limitations have been completed. Also all prophethoods, having arrived at their climax in the person of our lord and master, the Holy Prophet, peace and blessings of Allah be upon him, have been fulfilled.

The Reason for the Appearance of the Holy Prophet in Arabia

That the last Divine guidance should shine forth from Arabia was determined by Divine wisdom. The Arabs are descended from Ishmael who was cut asunder from Israel and had, under Divine wisdom, been cast into the wilderness of Paran (Faran), which means two fugitives. The descendants of Ishmael had been cut asunder from Bani Israel by Abraham himself and they had no part in the law of the Torah, as was written that they would not inherit from Isaac.

Thus they were abandoned by those to whom they belonged and had no relationship with anyone else. In all other countries there were some traces of worship and commandments which indicated that they had at one time received instruction from prophets. Arabia alone was a country that was utterly unacquainted with such teachings and was the most backward of all. Its turn came last of all and it received the benefit of a universal prophethood, so that all countries might share again in the blessings of prophethood, and the errors that had become current in the meantime among them might be weeded out. The Holy Quran is the Perfect Book which undertook the entire project of human reform and is not addressed only to one people. It seeks the reform of all and has set forth all grades of human development. It teaches savages the manners and ways of humanity and thereafter instructs them in high moral qualities. Thus there is no need of any other book beside the Holy Quran.

What the World Owes to the Holy Quran

It is a bounty of the Holy Quran upon mankind that it has set forth the distinction between man's natural state and moral qualities and that it does not stop merely at leading man from his natural conditions to the elevated palace of high moral qualities, but also opens the doors of the holy understanding that leads man to the spiritual heights. In this way it sets forth in an excellent manner the three types of teaching that we have already mentioned. As it comprehends all the teachings which are necessary for religious training, it claims it has discharged this function to perfection. It says:

$$\text{اَلْيَوْمَ اَكْمَلْتُ لَكُمْ دِيْنَكُمْ وَاَتْمَمْتُ عَلَيْكُمْ نِعْمَتِیْ وَ رَضِیْتُ لَكُمُ}$$

$$\text{الْاِسْلَامَ دِیْنًا ـ (المآئدة:٤)}$$

This day have I perfected your religion for your benefit, and have completed My favour unto you and have been pleased to appoint Islam as your religion (5:4). This means the climax of religion has been reached in Islam, which is that a person should be committed wholly to God and should seek his salvation through the sacrifice of his self in the cause of God, and not through any other means, and should demonstrate this motive and determination in his conduct. This is the stage at which all excellences arrive at their perfection. Thus, the Holy Quran has presented the God Who was not identified by the philosophers. The Quran has adopted two methods for the understanding of God. First, the method whereby human reason is strengthened and illumined for the purpose of setting forth reasons in support of the existence of God, and thus saves a person from falling into error. Secondly, the spiritual method which we shall set forth in answer to the third question.

Proof of the Existence of God

We now proceed to draw attention to the excellent and matchless proofs of the existence of God that the Holy Quran has set forth. At one place it has said:

$$\text{رَبُّنَا الَّذِىٓ اَعْطٰى كُلَّ شَىْءٍ خَلْقَهٗ ثُمَّ هَدٰى ـ (طه: ۵۱)}$$

Our Lord is He Who has bestowed upon everything its appropriate faculties, and has then guided it to the achievement of its appropriate purposes (20:51). If we keep in mind the purport of this verse and then reflect upon the shape and form of man and all the animals on land and in the sea, and the birds, we are impressed with the power of God Who has bestowed its appropriate form on everything. This is a vast subject and we would urge our listeners to reflect deeply upon it.

The second proof of the existence of God that the Holy Quran has set forth is that God is the ultimate cause of all causes, as it is said:

$$\text{وَاَنَّ اِلٰى رَبِّكَ الْمُنْتَهٰى ـ (النّجم: ۴۳)}$$

Thy Lord is the final cause of all causes (53:43). If we observe carefully we find that the entire universe is bound together in a system of cause and effect. This system is at the root of all knowledge. No part of creation is outside this system. Some things are the roots of others and some are branches. A cause may be primary or may be the effect of another cause, and that in its turn may be the effect of still another cause, and so on. Now, it is not possible that in this finite world this pattern of cause and effect should have no limit and should be infinite. We are compelled to acknowledge that it must terminate with some ultimate cause. The ultimate cause is God. This verse:

وَاَنَّ اِلٰى رَبِّكَ الْمُنْتَهٰى ـ (النَّجْم: ٤٣)

sets forth this argument very concisely and affirms that the system of cause and effect terminates in God (53:43).

Another proof of Divine existence set forth in the Quran is:

لَا الشَّمْسُ يَنْبَغِيْ لَهَآ اَنْ تُدْرِكَ الْقَمَرَ وَلَا

الَّيْلُ سَابِقُ النَّهَارِ وَكُلٌّ فِيْ فَلَكٍ يَّسْبَحُوْنَ ـ (يٰس: ٤١)

This means that the sun cannot catch up with the moon, and the night, which is a manifestation of the moon, cannot prevail over the day, which is a manifestation of the sun. Neither of them can move outside its orbit (36:41). Were there not a Regulator of the whole of this system behind the scenes, the system would fall into chaos. This proof is very striking in the estimation of astronomers. There are so many grand heavenly bodies that are gliding through space that the slightest disorder in their movements would bring about the ruin of the whole world. What a manifestation of Divine power is it that these bodies neither collide nor change their speed, nor alter their courses in the slightest degree, nor have they been worn out by their circulation during such a long period, nor has their machinery suffered any disorder. If they are not under the supervision of a Guardian, how is it that such a grand organisation continues to carry on through numberless years entirely on its own? At another place in the Quran God Almighty draws attention to this in the words:

اَفِی اللّٰهِ شَكٌّ فَاطِرِ السَّمٰوٰتِ وَالْاَرْضِ ، ابراهیم : ۱۱)

Can there be a doubt in the existence of God Who has originated the heavens and the earth (14:11)?

He has set forth another proof of His existence in the words:

كُلُّ مَنْ عَلَیْهَا فَانٍ. وَّیَبْقٰی وَجْهُ رَبِّكَ

ذُوالْجَلٰلِ وَ الْاِكْرَامِ ـ رالرّحمن : ۲۷-۲۸)

All that is on the earth will perish and only the countenance of thy Lord, Master of Glory and Honour, will survive (55:27-28). If we assume that the earth might be reduced into particles and the heavenly bodies might be broken down and everything might be overtaken by a blast that would wipe out every sign of these bodies, yet reason acknowledges and right conscience deems it necessary that after all this destruction there should survive One, Who is not subject to destruction, and can undergo no change and Who should continue in His pristine state. That One is God, Who has created everything mortal and is Himself immune from mortality.

Another proof of His existence that God has set forth in the Holy Quran is: God enquired from the souls:

اَلَسْتُ بِرَبِّكُمْ قَالُوْا بَلٰی ـ رالاعراف : ۱۷۳)

Am I not your Lord? and they answered: Indeed (7:173). In this verse God Almighty sets forth, in the form of question and answer, the characteristic with which He has invested the souls, and that is that by its very nature no soul can deny the existence of God. Those who deny God do so because they can find no proof of His existence according to their own fancy. Yet they acknowledge that for everything that is created there must be a creator. There is no one in the world so stupid that if he falls ill he would insist that there is no cause for his illness. If the system of the universe had not been made up of cause and effect, it would not have been possible to predict the time of a tornado, or of the eclipse of the sun or the moon, or that a patient would die at a certain time, or that a disease would be reinforced by another disease at a certain stage. Thus, a research scholar who does not acknowledge the existence of God, in effect does so indirectly, for he too, like us, searches for the causes of effects. This is an acknowledgment of a sort, though it is not perfect. Besides, if, through some device, a person who denies the existence of God could be made unconscious in such manner that he should pass under the complete control of God, discarding all fancies, emotions, and impulses of his earthly life, he would, in such a state, acknowledge the existence of God and would not deny it. This is testified to by eminent experts. The verse that we have cited also indicates that a denial of the existence of God is only a manifestation of this earthly existence, for the true nature of man fully confesses His existence.

Attributes of God

We have set forth these few proofs of the existence of God by way of illustration. We now call attention to the attributes of God to Whom the Holy Quran calls us, which are as follows:

هُوَ اللّٰهُ الَّذِىْ لَاۤ اِلٰهَ اِلَّا هُوَۚ عٰلِمُ الْغَيْبِ وَالشَّهَادَةِۚ

هُوَ الرَّحْمٰنُ الرَّحِيْمُ ـ (الحشر: ۲۳)

مٰلِكِ يَوْمِ الدِّيْنِ (الفاتحة: ٤)

اَلْمَلِكُ الْقُدُّوْسُ السَّلٰمُ الْمُؤْمِنُ الْمُهَيْمِنُ

الْعَزِيْزُ الْجَبَّارُ الْمُتَكَبِّرُ (الحشر: ٢٤)

هُوَ اللهُ الْخَالِقُ الْبَارِئُ الْمُصَوِّرُ لَهُ الْاَسْمَآءُ الْحُسْنٰي

يُسَبِّحُ لَهُ مَا فِى السَّمٰوٰتِ وَالْاَرْضِ وَهُوَ الْعَزِيْزُ

الْحَكِيْمُ - (الحشر: ٢٥)

اِنَّ اللهَ عَلٰي كُلِّ شَئْ قَدِيْرٌ - (البقرة: ٢١)

رَبِّ الْعٰلَمِيْنَ الرَّحْمٰنِ الرَّحِيْمِ مٰلِكِ يَوْمِ الدِّيْنِ (الفاتحة: ٢-٤)

اُجِيْبُ دَعْوَةَ الدَّاعِ اِذَا دَعَانِ - (البقرة: ١٨٧)

اَلْحَيُّ الْقَيُّوْمُ - (البقرة: ٢٥٦)

قُلْ هُوَ اللهُ اَحَدٌ- اَللهُ الصَّمَدُ- لَمْ يَلِدْ- وَلَمْ يُوْلَدْ

وَلَمْ يَكُنْ لَّهٗ كُفُوًا اَحَدٌ - (الاخلاص)

This means that God is One without associate and no one else beside Him is worthy of worship and obedience (59:23). This affirmation is made because, if He were not without associate, there might be an apprehension that He might be overcome by a rival, in which case Godhead would always be in peril. The affirmation that no one is worthy of worship beside Him means that He is so Perfect and His attributes are so excellent and exalted that if we were to select a god out of the universe who would be equipped with perfect attributes, or were to contemplate in our minds the best and most exalted attributes

that God should possess, He would be more exalted than all our
fancies. Whom no one can exceed and than Whom no one can be
more exalted. That is God, to associate anyone in Whose worship
would be the greatest wrong. He is the Knower of the unseen,
that is to say, He alone knows Himself. No one can comprehend
His Being. We can comprehend the sun and the moon in their
entirety, but we cannot comprehend God in His entirety. He is
the Knower of the seen, that is to say, nothing is hidden from
Him. It is not to be imagined that He should be unaware of
anything. He has every particle of the universe within His sight;
but man does not possess such comprehensive vision. He knows
when He might break up this system and bring about the
Judgment. No one else knows when that would happen. It is God
alone Who has knowledge of all those times. Then it is said: He is
the Gracious One (59:23). This means that before the coming
into being of animates and before any action proceeding from
them, out of His pure grace and not for any other purpose, nor as
a reward for any action, He makes due provision for everyone; as
for instance, He brought into being the sun and the earth and all
other things for our benefit before we came into being and before
any action had proceeded from us. This Divine bounty is
designated *Rahmaniyyat* in the Book of God, and on account of
it God Almighty is called *Rahman.* He rewards righteous action
richly and does not let go waste anyone's effort. On account of
this attribute He is called *Rahim,* and the attribute is designated
Rahimiyyat.

Then it is said:

مٰلِكِ يَوْمِ الدِّيْنِ (الفَاتِحَه : ٤)

He is Master of the Day of Judgment (1:4). This means that
He keeps the recompense of everyone in His own hand. He has
appointed no agent to whom He has committed the governance
of the heavens and the earth, having withdrawn from it

altogether, being no longer concerned with it, leaving to the agent the determination of all recompense at all times.

Then it is said:

اَلْمَلِكُ الْقُدُّوسُ ـ (الحشر: ٢٤)

He is the Sovereign without any default (59:24). It is obvious that human sovereignty is not without default. For instance, if all the subjects of an earthly sovereign were to leave their country and to migrate to another country, his sovereignty would come to an end. Or if all his people were afflicted with famine, how could any revenue be collected? Or if the people were to enquire from him what is it that he possesses beyond that which they possess on account of which they should obey him, what could he say in answer to their question? But God's sovereignty is not subject to any default. He can destroy everything in one instant and can create another kingdom. Had He not been such a Creator, possessing all power, His kingdom would not have endured without injustice. For instance, having forgiven and having bestowed salvation upon the people of the world once, how would He have acquired another world? Would He have sought to catch those upon whom He had already bestowed salvation so that He might send them back into the world, and would have revoked His forgiveness and salvation unjustly? In such case, His Godhead would have proved defective and He would have become an imperfect ruler like earthly sovereigns who frame ever new laws for their people and are put out of temper time after time; and when they find in their selfishness, that they cannot carry on without injustice, they have recourse to it without compunction. For instance, in terrestrial sovereignty it is considered permissible to let the passengers of a small vessel be destroyed in order to secure the safety of a large vessel, but God is under no such compulsion. If God had not been All-Powerful and had not the power to create out of nothing, He would have been compelled either to have recourse to injustice like weak sovereigns, or would have clung to justice and lost His Godhead. God's vessel continues its voyage with full power on the basis of justice.

Then He is the Source of Peace (59:24), that is to say, He is safeguarded against all defects, and misfortunes, and hardships, and provides security for all. If He had been liable to being afflicted with misfortunes, or to be killed by His people, or could have been frustrated in His designs, how could the hearts of people in such cases have been comforted by the conviction that he would deliver them from misfortunes?

God Almighty describes the condition of false gods in the following words:

$$\text{اِنَّ الَّذِيْنَ تَدْعُوْنَ مِنْ دُوْنِ اللهِ لَنْ يَّخْلُقُوْا ذُبَابًا}$$

$$\text{وَّلَوِ اجْتَمَعُوْا لَهٗ ؕ وَاِنْ يَّسْلُبْهُمُ الذُّبَابُ شَيْئًا}$$

$$\text{لَّا يَسْتَنْقِذُوْهُ مِنْهُ ؕ ضَعُفَ الطَّالِبُ وَالْمَطْلُوْبُ ۔}$$

$$\text{مَا قَدَرُوا اللهَ حَقَّ قَدْرِهٖ ؕ اِنَّ اللهَ لَقَوِيٌّ عَزِيْزٌ ۔}$$

(الحج: ٧٤-٧٥)

Those on whom you call beside Allah cannot create even a fly, though they should all combine together for the purpose; and if a fly should snatch away anything from them, they cannot recover it therefrom. Their worshippers lack intelligence and they themselves lack power. Can such as these be gods? God is One Who is more powerful than all those who possess power. He is the Mighty, Who is supreme over all. No one can apprehend Him or kill Him. Those who fall into such errors have not a true concept of God's attributes (22:74-75).

Then God is the Bestower of Security and sets forth proof of His attributes and His Unity. This is an indication that he who believes in the True God is not embarrassed in any company, nor would he be remorseful in the presence of God, for he is equipped with strong proofs. But he who believes in a false god finds himself in great distress. He describes every senseless thing as a mystery so that he should not be laughed at and seeks to hide demonstrable errors.

Then He is

$$\text{الْمُهَيْمِنُ الْعَزِيزُ الْجَبَّارُ الْمُتَكَبِّرُ} -$$

the Protector, the Mighty, the Subduer, the Exalted. This means that He safeguards all and is supreme over all and sets right all that might have gone wrong and is completely Self-Sufficient (59:24).

$$\text{هُوَ اللهُ الْخَالِقُ الْبَارِئُ الْمُصَوِّرُ لَهُ الْأَسْمَاءُ الْحُسْنَى}$$

$$\text{يُسَبِّحُ لَهُ مَا فِى السَّمٰوٰتِ وَالْأَرْضِ وَهُوَ الْعَزِيزُ}$$

$$\text{الْحَكِيمُ}$$

He is Allah, the Creator, the Maker, the Fashioner; His are the most beautiful names. All that is in the heavens and the earth glorifies Him. He is the Mighty, the Wise (59:25). This means that He is the Creator of the bodies as well as of the souls. He determines the features of a baby in the womb. To Him belong all the beautiful names that can be thought of.

The dwellers of the heaven and the dwellers of the earth glorify Him. This is an indication that the heavenly bodies are also populated and their dwellers follow Divine guidance.

$$اِنَّ اللّٰهَ عَلٰی کُلِّ شَیْءٍ قَدِیْرٌ - (البقرة : ۲۱)$$

He has the power to do all that He wills (2:21). This provides great comfort for His worshippers, for what can be expected of a god who is weak and without power?

Then it is said:

$$رَبِّ الْعٰلَمِیْنَ الرَّحْمٰنِ الرَّحِیْمِ مٰلِکِ یَوْمِ الدِّیْنِ (الفاتحة: ۲-٤)$$

$$اُجِیْبُ دَعْوَةَ الدَّاعِ اِذَا دَعَانِ (البقرة : ۱۸۷)$$

He is the Lord of the worlds, Most Gracious, Ever Merciful, Master of the Day of judgment (1:2-4). This means that He provides for the universe and is Himself the Master of the Day of Judgment and has not committed Judgment to anyone else.

Then it is said: I respond to the call of him who calls on Me (2:187),

$$اَلْحَیُّ الْقَیُّوْمُ - (البقرة : ۲۵٦)$$

the Ever-Living, the Self-Subsisting, and the Self-Sufficient (2:256). The life of every life, and the support of every being. He is the Ever-Living, for if He were not Ever-Living, His worshippers would be apprehensive lest He should die before them.

Then it is said: Proclaim: He is Allah, the Single. He begets not, nor is He begotten; and there is no one who is His equal or like unto Him (112:2-5).

To believe in the Unity of God correctly, without the least deviation, is the justice that is due from a man towards his Maker. We have set out the moral teachings of Islam from the Holy Quran, the basic principle of which is that there should be neither excess nor deficiency; it is the characteristic of a moral quality that it does not exceed or fall short of its appropriate limit. It is obvious that virtue lies in the middle of two extremes.

Only that habit which seeks to establish itself in the middle promotes a high moral quality. To recognize the proper place and occasion is itself a middle. For instance, if a farmer does his sowing too early or too late, he departs from the middle. Virtue and truth and wisdom are the middle and the middle is appropriateness; in other words truth is always in the middle of two opposing falsehoods. There is no doubt that watchfulness for the proper occasion keeps a person in the middle. Keeping to the middle in relation to God means that in expounding Divine attributes one should not lean towards negating Divine attributes nor describe God as resembling material things. This is the way that the Holy Quran has adopted with reference to Divine attributes. It affirms that God sees, hears, knows, speaks; and as a safeguard against His being understood as resembling His creation it also affirms:

$$ لَيْسَ كَمِثْلِهِ شَىْءٌ ۚ - ر الشورى، ١٢ ）$$

$$ فَلَا تَضْرِبُوْا لِلّٰهِ الْاَمْثَالَ - رالنَّحل، ٧٥ ）$$

There is nothing like unto Him (42:12); and Fabricate not similitudes concerning God (16:75). This means that there is no partner in the Being and attributes of God and that He bears no resemblance to His creatures. To conceive of God as being between resemblance and transcendence is the proper middle. In short all Islamic teachings observe the middle. The Surah Fatiha also inculcates adherence to the middle. It teaches the supplication to be guided along the path of those on whom God has bestowed His favours, and not of those who have incurred His wrath, nor of those who have gone astray (1:7). By those who incurred His wrath are meant people who in juxtaposition to God yield to the wrathful faculty and act savagely; and by those who have gone astray are meant people who behave like animals. The middle way is that which has been described as the way of those on whom God has bestowed His favours. In short, for this blessed people the Holy Quran has prescribed adherence to the middle. In the Torah God Almighty had laid emphasis on retribution, and in the Gospel He laid emphasis on forbearance and forgiveness. The Muslims have been directed to seek appropriateness and to ahdere to the middle; as is said:

وَكَذٰلِكَ جَعَلْنٰكُمْ اُمَّةً وَّسَطًا - (البقرة : ١٤٤)

Thus have We made you the people of the middle (2:144), meaning that the Muslims have been directed to keep to the middle. Thus blessed are those who proceed along the middle.

خَـيْرُ الْاُمُوْرِ اَوْسَطُهَا۔

The middle is the best.

Spiritual Conditions

The third question is: What are spiritual conditions? We have already stated that according to the Holy Quran the fountainhead of spiritual conditions is the soul at rest, which carries a person from the grade of a moral being to the grade of a godly being, as Allah, the Glorious, has said:

يٰٓاَيَّتُهَا النَّفْسُ الْمُطْمَئِنَّةُ ارْجِعِىْٓ اِلٰى رَبِّكِ رَاضِيَةً مَّرْضِيَّةً ۔

فَادْخُلِىْ فِىْ عِبَادِىْ۔ وَادْخُلِىْ جَنَّتِىْ ۔ (الفجر : ٢٨-٣١)

O soul that has found its rest in God, return to thy Lord, thou well pleased with Him and He well pleased with thee. So enter among My chosen servants and enter My Garden (89:28-31).

It should be remembered that the highest spiritual condition of a person in this life is that he should find comfort in God and all his satisfaction, and ecstasy and delight should be centered in God. This is the condition which is called the heavenly life. In this condition a person is bestowed the heavenly life in this very world in return for his perfect sincerity, purity and faithfulness. Other people look forward to paradise in the hereafter, but he enters it in this very life. Arriving at this stage a person realizes that the worship that was prescribed for him is in truth the food that nurtures his soul, and on which his spiritual life largely depends, and that its consummation is not postponed to the after life. All the reproof that the reproving self administers to him on his unclean life and yet fails to rouse fully his longing for virtue and to generate real disgust against his evil desires, and to bestow full power of adherence to virtue, is transformed by this urge which is the beginning of the development of the soul at rest. On arriving at this stage a person becomes capable of achieving complete prosperity. All the passions of self begin to wither and a strengthening breeze begins to blow upon the soul so that the person concerned looks upon his previous weaknesses with remorse. At that time nature and habits experience a complete transformation and the person is drawn far away from his previous condition. He is washed and cleansed and God inscribes love of virtue upon his heart and casts out from it the impurity of vice with His own hand. The forces of truth all enter the citadel of his heart and righteousness occupies all the battlements of his nature, and truth becomes victorious and falsehood lays down its arms and is put to flight. The hand of God is placed over his heart and he takes every step under the shade of God. God Almighty has indicated all this in the following verses:

اُولٰٓئِكَ كَتَبَ فِیۡ قُلُوۡبِهِمُ الۡاِیۡمَانَ وَاَیَّدَهُمۡ بِرُوۡحٍ

مِّنۡهُ ۖ - ﴿المجادلة:۲۳﴾

حَبَّبَ اِلَیۡكُمُ الۡاِیۡمَانَ وَ زَیَّنَهٗ فِیۡ قُلُوۡبِكُمۡ وَكَرَّهَ اِلَیۡكُمُ

الْكُفْرَ وَالْفُسُوقَ وَالْعِصْيَانَ اُولَٰئِكَ هُمُ الرَّاشِدُونَ

فَضْلًا مِّنَ اللّٰهِ وَنِعْمَةً ۚ وَاللّٰهُ عَلِيْمٌ حَكِيْمٌ ۔ (الحجرات: ٨-٩)

جَآءَ الْحَقُّ وَزَهَقَ الْبَاطِلُ إِنَّ الْبَاطِلَ كَانَ

زَهُوْقًا ۔ (بنی اسرائیل: ٨٢)

These are they in whose hearts Allah has inscribed faith with
His own hand and whom He has helped with the Holy Spirit
(58:23). Allah has endeared faith to you and has made it to seem
fair to your hearts, and He has made you averse to disbelief,
wickedness and disobedience and impressed upon your hearts the
viciousness of evil ways. All this has come about through the
grace and favour of Allah. Allah is All-Knowing Wise (49:8-9).
Truth has arrived and falsehood has vanished, falsehood is bound
to disappear (17:82).

All this pertains to the spiritual condition which a person
attains at the third stage. No one can acquire true insight unless
he arrives at this condition. God's inscribing faith on their hearts
with His own hand and helping them with the Holy Spirit means
that no one can achieve true purity and righteousness unless he
receives heavenly help. At the stage of the reproving self a
person's condition is that he repents time after time and yet falls
down and often despairs and considers his condition beyond
remedy. He remains in this situation for a period and when the
appointed time comes a light during the day. With the descent of
that light he undergoes a wonderful change and he perceives the
control of a hidden hand, and beholds a wonderful world. At that
time he realizes that God exists and his eyes are filled with a light
which they did not possess before.

How shall we discover that path and how shall we acquire that light? Be it known that in this world every effect has a cause and behind every move there is a mover. For the acquisition of every type of knowledge there is appointed a way that is called the straight path. Nothing can be achieved in this world without conformity to the rules that nature has appointed in that behalf from the very beginning. The law of nature informs us that for the achievement of each purpose there is appointed a straight path and the purpose can be achieved only by following that path. For instance, if we are sitting in a dark room, the straight path for obtaining the light of the sun is for us to open the window that faces the sun. When we do that, the light of the sun instantly enters the room and illumines it. Thus it is obvious that for the acquisition of God's love and real grace there must be some window, and there must be an appointed method for the acquisition of pure spirituality. Then we should see the straight path that leads to spirituality as we seek a straight path for the achievement of all our other purposes. That method is not that we should seek to meet God only through the exercise of our reason and by following our self-appointed ways. The doors which can only be opened by His powerful hands will not yield to our logic and philosophy. We cannot find the Ever-Living and Self-Subsisting God through our own devices. The only straight path for the achievement of this purpose is that we should first devote our lives, together with all our faculties, to the cause of God Almighty, and should then occupy ourselves with supplication for meeting Him, and should thus find God through God Himself.

An Excellent Prayer

The most excellent prayer which instructs us concerning the time and occasion of supplication and depicts before us the picture of spiritual zeal is the one that God, the Beneficent, has taught us in the opening chapter of the Holy Quran. It is as follows:

$$\text{بِسْمِ اللهِ الرَّحْمٰنِ الرَّحِيْمِ ـ اَلْحَمْدُ لِلّٰهِ رَبِّ الْعٰلَمِيْنَ ـ}$$

All worthiness of praise belongs to Allah alone Who is the Creator and Sustainer of all the worlds (1:2)

$$\text{الرَّحْمٰنِ الرَّحِيْمِ ـ}$$

He provides for us out of His mercy before any action proceeds from us, and after we have acted He rewards our action out of His mercy (1:3).

$$\text{مٰلِكِ يَوْمِ الدِّيْنِ ـ}$$

He alone is the Master of the Day of Judgment and has not committed that day to anyone else (1:4).

$$\text{اِيَّاكَ نَعْبُدُ وَاِيَّاكَ نَسْتَعِيْنُ ـ}$$

O Thou Who dost comprehend all these attributes, we worship Thee alone and seek Thy help in all our affairs (1:5). The use of the plural pronoun in this context indicates that all our faculties are occupied in His worship and are prostrate at His threshold. Every person by virtue of his inner faculties is a multiple entity and the prostration of all his faculties before God is the condition that is called Islam.

$$\text{اِهْدِنَا الصِّرَاطَ الْمُسْتَقِيْمَ ـ صِرَاطَ الَّذِيْنَ اَنْعَمْتَ عَلَيْهِمْ ـ}$$

Guide us along Thy straight path and establish us firmly on it (1:6); the path of those upon whom Thou hast bestowed Thy bounties and favours,

$$\text{غَيْرِ الْمَغْضُوْبِ عَلَيْهِمْ وَلَا الضَّآلِّيْنَ ـ}$$

and not of those who have incurred Thy wrath, nor of those who went astray and did not reach Thee (1:7). Amen.

These verses tell us that divine bounties and favours are bestowed only upon those who offer up their lives as a sacrifice in the cause of God, and devoting themselves wholly to it and being occupied entirely with His pleasure continue to supplicate so that they might be bestowed all the spiritual bounties that a human being can receive by way of nearness to God, meeting Him and hearing His words. With this supplication they worship God through all their faculties, eschew sin and remain prostrate at His threshold. They safeguard themselves against all vice and shun the ways of God's wrath. As they seek God with high resolve and perfect sincerity, they find Him and are given to drink their fill of their understanding of God. The true and perfect grace that conveys a person to the spiritual world depends upon steadfastness, by which is meant that degree of sincerity and faithfulness which cannot be shaken by any trial. It means a strong relationship with the Divine which a sword cannot cut asunder and fire cannot consume, nor can any other calamity damage it. The death of dear ones or separation from them should not interfere with it, nor should fear of dishonour affect it, nor should a painful death move the heart away from it in the least degree. Thus this door is very narrow and this path is very hard. Alas how difficult it is!

This is indicated by Almighty God in the following verse:

قُلْ اِنْ كَانَ اٰبَآؤُكُمْ وَاَبْنَآؤُكُمْ وَاِخْوَانُكُمْ وَاَزْوَاجُكُمْ
وَعَشِيْرَتُكُمْ وَاَمْوَالُ اِقْتَرَفْتُمُوْهَا وَتِجَارَةٌ تَخْشَوْنَ
كَسَادَهَا وَمَسٰكِنُ تَرْضَوْنَهَآ اَحَبَّ اِلَيْكُمْ مِّنَ اللّٰهِ
وَرَسُوْلِهٖ وَجِهَادٍ فِيْ سَبِيْلِهٖ فَتَرَبَّصُوْا حَتّٰى يَاْتِيَ

اللهُ بِأَمْرِهِ وَاللهُ لَا يَهْدِى الْقَوْمَ الْفَاسِقِيْنَ ـ (التوبه : ٢٤)

Tell them: If your fathers, and your sons, and your brethren, and your wives, and your kinsfolk, and the wealth that you have acquired, and the trade the dullness of which you apprehend, and the dwellings that you fancy, are dearer to you than Allah and His Messenger and striving in His cause, then wait until Allah declares His judgment. Allah guides not the disobedient people (9:24).

This verse clearly shows that those people who put aside the will of God and give preference to their relatives and their properties whom they love better, are evil-doers in the estimation of God and that they would surely be ruined because they preferred something else to God. This is the third stage in which that person becomes godly. Such a person welcomes thousands of calamities for the sake of God, and leans towards Him with such sincerity and devotion as if he has no one related to him except God, and all others have died. The truth is that till we submit ourselves to death we cannot behold the Living God. The day our physical life undergoes death is the day of the manifestation of God. We are blind till we become blind to the sight of all besides God. We are dead till we become like a corpse in the hand of God. It is only when we face God completely that we acquire the steadfastness that overcomes all passions of self, and that steadfastness brings about the death of the life that is devoted to selfish purposes. This is described in the verse:

بَلَى مَنْ أَسْلَمَ وَجْهَهُ لِلّٰهِ وَهُوَ مُحْسِنٌ ـ (البقرة: ١١٣)

This means that God requires that we should offer ourselves to be sacrificed in His cause (2:113). We shall achieve steadfastness when all our faculties and powers are devoted to His cause and our life and our death are all for His sake, as He has said:

قُلْ اِنَّ صَلَاتِیْ وَنُسُکِیْ وَ مَحْیَایَ وَ مَمَاتِیْ لِلّٰهِ رَبِّ الْعٰلَمِیْنَ ۔ (الانعام:۱۶۳)

Proclaim, O Prophet: My prayer and my sacrifices and my living and my dying are all for the sake of Allah (6:163).

When a person's love of God reaches a stage at which his living and his dying is not for his own sake but is entirely for God, then God, Who has always loved those who love Him, bestows His love upon him and by the meeting of these two loves a light is generated inside the person which the world cannot recognize or understand. Thousands of the righteous and the elect had to lay down their lives because the world did not recognize them. They were accounted selfish and deceitful as the world could not see their bright countenances, as is said:

یَنْظُرُوْنَ اِلَیْکَ وَ هُمْ لَا یُبْصِرُوْنَ ۔ (الاعراف ۱۹۹)

They look at thee, but they do not see thee (7:199).

In short, from the day when that light is generated in a person, he ceases to be earthly and becomes heavenly. He Who is the Master of all beings speaks inside him and manifests the light of His Godhead and makes his heart, which is saturated with His love, His throne. As soon as such a one becomes a new person through His bright transformation, God becomes a new God for him and manifests new ways for him. It is not that God becomes another God, or that those ways are different from His ways, and yet they are distinct from His normal ways, of which worldly philosophy is not aware. He becomes one of those who are referred to in the verse:

وَ مِنَ النَّاسِ مَنْ یَّشْرِیْ نَفْسَهُ ابْتِغَآءَ مَرْضَاتِ اللّٰهِ
وَ اللّٰهُ رَءُوْفٌ بِالْعِبَادِ ۔ (البقرة:۲۰۸)

Of the people there are those of high degree who dedicate themselves wholly to seeking the pleasure of Allah in return for their lives. These are the people towards whom Allah is Most Compassionate (2:208). Thus he who arrives at the stage of spiritual life becomes wholly devoted to the cause of Allah.

In this verse God Almighty sets forth that only such a one is delivered from all suffering who sells his life in the cause of Allah in return for His pleasure and proves his devotion by laying down his life. He considers that he has been brought into being for obedience to his Creator and for service of his fellow beings. He performs all the virtues which are related to every one of his faculties with such eagerness and sincerity as if he beholds his True Beloved in the mirror of his obedience. His will is identified with the Will of God and all his delight is centered in his obedience to God. Righteous conduct proceeds from him not as labour but as delight and pleasure. This is the paradise that is bestowed upon a spiritual person in this very life. The paradise that will be bestowed in the hereafter would be a reflection of this paradise which will, through Divine power, be manifested physically. This is referred to in the following verses:

وَلِمَنْ خَافَ مَقَامَ رَبِّهِ جَنَّتٰنِ ﴿الرَّحْمٰن: ٤٧﴾

وَسَقٰهُمْ رَبُّهُمْ شَرَابًا طَهُورًا ﴿الدهر: ٢٢﴾

إِنَّ الْأَبْرَارَ يَشْرَبُونَ مِنْ كَأْسٍ كَانَ مِزَاجُهَا

كَافُورًا. عَيْنًا يَشْرَبُ بِهَا عِبَادُ اللهِ يُفَجِّرُونَهَا

تَفْجِيرًا. ﴿الدهر: ٦،٧﴾

وَيُسْقَوْنَ فِيهَا كَأْسًا كَانَ مِزَاجُهَا زَنْجَبِيلًا ﴿الدهر ١٨﴾

عَيْنًا فِيهَا تُسَمّٰى سَلْسَبِيلًا ﴿الدهر: ١٩﴾

إِنَّا أَعْتَدْنَا لِلْكَافِرِينَ سَلَاسِلَ وَأَغْلَالًا وَسَعِيرًا ﴿الدهر: ٥﴾

وَمَنْ كَانَ فِى هٰذِهٖ اَعْمٰى فَهُوَ فِى الْاٰخِرَةِ اَعْمٰى وَاَضَلُّ سَبِيْلًا ـ (بنی اسرائیل: ۷۳)

For him who fears to stand before his Lord and is in awe of His Greatness and Majesty, there are two gardens, one in this world and the other in the hereafter (55:47). Those who are wholly devoted to God will be given a drink that will purify their hearts and their thoughts and their designs (76:22). The virtuous shall be given a drink which is tempered with camphor, from a spring wherefrom the servants of Allah drink. They cause it to gush forth through their own efforts (76:6-7).

The meaning of drinks prepared from camphor and ginger

We have already explained that the word *Kafoor* has been used in this verse for this reason that the Arabic word *kafara* means suppression and covering up. This is an indication that these people have quaffed the cup of cutting asunder from the world and turning to God with such sincerity that their love of the world has become quite cold. It is well known that all passions originate in the heart and when the heart withdraws altogether from all undesirable fancies and never reverts to them at all, those passions begin to decline till they disappear altogether; that is what is conveyed in this verse, that is to say, that such people draw far away from the passions of self and incline so completely towards God that their hearts become cold to worldly pursuits and their passions are suppressed as camphor suppresses poisonous matter.

Then it is said: They will be given to drink therein of a cup tempered with ginger (76:18-19). The Arabic word for ginger *(Zanjabil)* is a compound of *zana* and *jabal*. *Zana* in Arabic idiom means ascending and *jabal* means a mountain, thus *Zanajabal* means: He ascends the mountain. It should be remembered that after a person recovers from a poisonous disease he passes through two stages before he is restored to full health and strength. The first stage is when the poisonous matter is completely overcome and dangerous tendencies are reformed and poisonous conditions are safely averted and the attack of the fatal upsurge is completely suppressed, but the limbs are still weak, strength is lacking and the patient treads wearily. The second stage is when the patient is restored to full health and his body achieves full strength and he feels that he can climb hills and run along the heights. This condition is achieved in the third stage concerning which God Almighty has said that godly people of the highest rank drink of cups that are flavoured with ginger; that is to say, that arriving at the full strength of their spiritual condition they can climb high mountains; meaning that they carry out great projects and make great sacrifices in the cause of God.

The effect of ginger
It should be remembered that one of the qualities of ginger is that it strengthens the system and relieves dysentery and warms it up so that a person becomes capable, as it were, of climbing a mountain. By placing camphor and ginger in juxtaposition it is intended to convey that when a person moves from a condition of subordination to his passions towards virtue, the first reaction is that the poisonous matters from which he suffers are suppressed and the surge of passions begins to subside as camphor suppresses poisonous matters. That is why it is found useful in the treatment of cholera and typhoid. When poisonous matters are completely suppressed and the patient recovers his health to a degree in which he still feels weak, the second stage is that he derives strength from a drink flavoured with ginger. In spiritual terms this drink is the manifestation of divine beauty which is the nourishment of the soul. When he derives strength from this manifestation he is enabled to climb high mountains, that is to say, he performs such surprisingly difficult feats in the cause of

God that no one whose heart is not inspired by the warmth of love can perform. In these verses God Almighty has employed two Arabic terms to illustrate these two conditions; one term is camphor which means suppression and the other is ginger which means climbing. These are the two conditions which are encountered by seekers after God.

$$ إِنَّا أَعْتَدْنَا لِلْكَافِرِينَ سَلَاسِلَاْ وَأَغْلَالًا وَسَعِيرًا $$

(الدهر: ٥)

We have prepared chains and collars and a blazing fire for the disbelievers (76:5). This means that for those who reject the truth and have no inclination towards accepting it, God has prepared chains and collars and a blazing fire. The meaning is that those who do not seek God with a true heart suffer a severe reaction. They are so much involved with the world as if their feet are secured by chains, and they bend down so much towards worldly pursuits as if there are collars round their necks which do not permit them to lift their eyes towards heaven. They have a burning desire for the things of the world, property, authority, domination, wealth, etc. As God Almighty finds them unworthy and committed to undesirable pursuits He inflicts them with these three sufferings. This is an indication that every human action is followed by a corresponding action on the part of God. For instance, when a person closes all the doors and windows of his room, his action is followed by a Divine action whereby the room becomes dark. All the inevitable consequences of our actions that have been appointed by God Almighty under the law of nature are all God's actions, inasmuch as He is the Cause of causes. For instance, if a person swallows poison, his action would be followed by the Divine action that he would suffer death. In the same way if a person acts in some improper way which attracts an infectious disease, his action would be followed by the Divine

action that he would be afflicted with that disease. Thus, as we
observe clearly that in our wordly life, there is an inevitable result
for every action of ours, and that result is the act of God
Almighty, the same law operates in religious matters also. For
instance, it is said:

$$وَالَّذِيْنَ جَاهَدُوْا فِيْنَا لَنَهْدِيَنَّهُمْ سُبُلَنَا (العنكبوت:٧٠)$$

$$فَلَمَّا زَاغُوْا اَزَاغَ اللهُ قُلُوْبَهُمْ (الصف:٦)$$

This means that in consequence of the full striving of a person
in seeking God, the inevitable act of God is to guide him along
the ways that lead to Him (29:70). As a contrast it is said: When
they deviated from the right course and did not desire to tread
along the straight path, the Divine action followed in that their
hearts were made perverse (61:6). To illustrate this even more
clearly it is said:

$$وَمَنْ كَانَ فِيْ هٰذِهٖ اَعْمٰى فَهُوَ فِي الْاٰخِرَةِ اَعْمٰى وَاَضَلُّ$$

$$سَبِيْلًا ـ (بنى اسرآءيل:٧٣)$$

He who remains blind in this life will be blind in the hereafter
also, and even more astray (17:73). This is an indication that the
virtuous see God in this very life and they behold their True
Beloved in this world. The purport of this verse is that the
foundation of the heavenly life is laid in this very world and that
the root of hellish blindness is also the vile and blind life of this
world.

Then it is said:

$$وَبَشِّرِ الَّذِيْنَ اٰمَنُوْا وَعَمِلُوا الصّٰلِحٰتِ اَنَّ لَهُمْ جَنّٰتٍ$$

$$تَجْرِيْ مِنْ تَحْتِهَا الْاَنْهٰرُ ـ (البقرة:٢٤)$$

Give glad tidings to those who believe and work righteousness, that for them there are gardens beneath which rivers flow (2:26). In this verse God Almighty has described faith as a garden beneath which rivers flow, and has thus indicated that faith is related to righteous action as a garden is related to the water of the river or stream. As a garden cannot flourish without water, faith cannot survive without righteous action. If there is faith but no righteous action the faith is vain; and if there are actions but not faith, the actions are mere show or display. The reality of the Islamic paradise is that it is a reflection of the faith and actions of a person in this life and is not something that will be bestowed upon a person from outside. A person's paradise is developed inside him and everyone's paradise is his faith and his righteous actions, the delight of which begins to be tasted in this very life and one perceives the hidden gardens and streams of faith and righteous action which will become concretely manifest in the hereafter. God's holy teaching instructs us that pure and perfect and firm faith in God, His attributes and His designs, is a beautiful garden of fruit trees, and righteous actions are the streams that irrigate the garden. The Holy Quran says:

$$ ضَرَبَ اللّٰهُ مَثَلًا كَلِمَةً طَيِّبَةً كَشَجَرَةٍ طَيِّبَةٍ اَصْلُهَا ثَابِتٌ $$

$$ وَّفَرْعُهَا فِى السَّمَآءِ تُؤْتِىٓ اُكُلَهَا كُلَّ حِيْنٍ ـ رابرهيمِ: ٢٥-٢٧ $$

This means that a word of faith which is free from every extreme and defect and falsehood and vanity and is perfect in every way, is like a tree which is free from every defect. The root of that tree is firm in the earth and its branches spread into heaven. It brings forth its fruit at all times and at no time are its branches without fruit (14:25-26). Thus it will be seen that God

Almighty has described a word of faith as a tree that bears fruit at all times and has set forth three of its characteristics.

The first is that its root, that is to say, its true meaning should be firm in the earth, meaning that its truth and reality should be acceptable to human nature and conscience.

Its second characteristic is that its branches should spread out into heaven, meaning that it should be supported by reason and should be in accord with the heavenly law of nature which is the work of God. In other words, the law of nature should furnish arguments in support of its correctness and truth, and those arguments should be beyond the reach of criticism.

Its third characteristic should be that its fruit should be permanent and unlimited, that is to say, the blessings and effects of acting upon it should continue to be manifested at all times and should not cease to be manifested after a period.

Then it is said:

$$ وَمَثَلُ كَلِمَةٍ خَبِيثَةٍ كَشَجَرَةٍ خَبِيثَةٍ اجْتُثَّتْ $$

$$ مِنْ فَوْقِ الْأَرْضِ مَا لَهَا مِنْ قَرَارٍ - ١ابراهيم:٢٧) $$

The case of an evil word is like that of an evil tree, which is uprooted from the earth and has no stability (14:27); meaning that human nature rejects it and it cannot be established by reason, or the law of nature or human conscience. It has no more stability than an idle tale. As the Holy Quran has said that the trees of true faith will appear in the hereafter as grapes and pomegranates and other good fruits, in the same way the evil tree of faithlessness is called *Zaqqum*, as is said:

$$ اَذٰلِكَ خَيْرٌ نُزُلاً اَمْ شَجَرَةُ الزَّقُّومِ. اِنَّا جَعَلْنَاهَا فِتْنَةً $$

$$ لِلظَّالِمِينَ اِنَّهَا شَجَرَةٌ تَخْرُجُ فِيْ اَصْلِ الْجَحِيْمِ طَلْعُهَا $$

كَأَنَّهُ رُءُوسُ الشَّيَاطِينِ ـ (الصَّفَّت: ٦٣ ـ ٦٦)

إِنَّ شَجَرَتَ الزَّقُّومِ طَعَامُ الْأَثِيمِ كَالْمُهْلِ يَغْلِى فِى

الْبُطُونِ كَغَلْىِ الْحَمِيمِ ـ (الدُّخان: ٤٤ ـ ٤٧)

ذُقْ إِنَّكَ أَنْتَ الْعَزِيزُ الْكَرِيمُ ـ (الدُّخان: ٥٠)

Are the gardens of paradise better entertainment or the tree *Zaqqum* which We have made a means of trial for the wrongdoers? It is a tree that springs forth from the root of hell, that is to say, it grows out of arrogance and self-esteem. Its fruit is, as if it were, the heads of Satan, meaning that he who eats it would be ruined (37:63-66). Then it is said: The tree of *Zaqqum* is the food of the deliberately sinful. It will boil in their bellies like molten copper (44:44-47). The sinful one will be commanded: Now suffer this, thou who didst hold thyself mighty and noble (44:51). This is a wrathful expression meaning that if he had not been arrogant and had not turned away from the truth out of pride and a false notion of his dignity, he would not have had to suffer in this fashion. This verse indicates that the word *Zaqqum* is compounded of *Zuq*, meaning, taste it, and *am* which is formed by the first and last letters of the remaining portion of the verse.

ذُقْ إِنَّكَ أَنْتَ الْعَزِيزُ الْكَرِيمُ ـ (الدُّخان: ٥٠)

Thus, God Almighty has described the words of faith uttered in this life as the trees of paradise. In the same way He has described the words of faithlessness uttered in this life as the tree of hell which He has called *Zaqqum*, and has thus indicated that the root of paradise and of hell is laid in this very life.

At another place hell is described as:

نَارُ اللهِ الْمُوقَدَةُ الَّتِى تَطَّلِعُ عَلَى الْأَفْئِدَةِ (الهُمَزَة: ٧ ـ ٨)

meaning that hell is a fire the source of which is the wrath of God and which is kindled by sin and overcomes the heart (104:7-8). This is an indication that at the root of this fire are the sorrows and griefs and torments which afflict the heart. All spiritual torments arise in the heart and then envelop the whole body. At another place it is said:

$$ \text{(٢٥ : وَقُودُهَا النَّاسُ وَ الْحِجَارَةُ ــ رالبقرة)} $$

meaning that the fuel of the fire of hell which keeps it blazing is of two types. One, those men who turn away from God and worship other things, or who require their own worship; as is said:

$$ \text{(٩٩:الانبياء) إِنَّكُمْ وَمَا تَعْبُدُونَ مِنْ دُونِ اللهِ حَصَبُ جَهَنَّمَ} $$

meaning that false deities and their worshippers will all be thrown into hell. The second type of fuel of hell is the idols. If there had been no false gods and no idols, nor any worshippers of these, there would have been no hell (2:25; 21:99).

All these verses show that in the Holy word of God, heaven and hell are not like the physical world. Their source is spiritual, though it is true that in the hereafter they will take on concrete forms and yet they will not belong to this world.

Means of Establishing Perfect Spiritual Relationship with God

The method of establishing perfect spiritual relationship with God that the Holy Quran teaches us is Islam, meaning devoting one's whole life to the cause of God and being occupied with the supplications which we have been taught in Surah Fatiha. This is the essence of Islam. Complete surrender to God and the supplication taught in Surah Fatiha are the only methods of meeting God and drinking the water of true salvation. This is the only method that the law of nature has appointed for man's highest exaltation and for his meeting the Divine. Those alone find God who enter into the spiritual fire of Islam and continue occupied with the supplication set out in Surah Fatiha. Islam is the blazing fire that burns up our life and, consuming our false deities, presents the sacrifice of our life and our property and our honour to our Holy God. Entering it, we drink the water of a new life and all our spiritual faculties establish such a relationship with God as subsists between kindred. A fire leaps up from our inside like lightning and another fire descends upon us from above. By the meeting of these two flames all our passions and our love for anything beside God are totally consumed and we become dead vis-a-vis our previous life. This condition is named Islam in the Holy Quran. Through our complete surrender to the will of God our passions are killed, and through supplication we acquire new life. This second life is signalised by the receipt of revelation. Arriving at this stage is interpreted as meeting with God, in other words beholding God. At this stage, a person establishes a relationship with God by virtue of which he becomes as if he were beholding God, and he is invested with power and all his senses and his inner faculties are illumined and he feels the strong pull of a holy life. At this stage, God becomes his eye with which he sees, and becomes his tongue with which he speaks, and becomes his hand with which he assaults his enemy, and becomes his ear with which he hears, and becomes his feet with which he walks. This stage is referred to in the verse:

$$ يَدُ اللهِ فَوْقَ اَيْدِيْهِمْ ۚ ـ (الفتح: ١١) $$

Allah's hand is above their hands (48:11). In the same way it is said:

$$ وَ مَا رَمَيْتَ اِذْ رَمَيْتَ وَ لٰكِنَّ اللهَ رَمٰى ۚ ـ (الانفال: ١٨) $$

It was not thou who didst throw, but it was Allah Who threw (8:18). In short, at this stage there is perfect union with God and

His holy Will pervades the soul thoroughly, and the moral power
that had previously been weak becomes firm like a mountain and
reason and intelligence are sharpened to the extreme. This is the
meaning of the verse:

$$ وَ اَيَّدَهُمْ بِرُوْحٍ مِّنْهُ ۚ (المجادله ٢٣) $$

He has strengthened them with His spirit (58:23). At this stage
the streams of love for and devotion to Him surge up in such
manner that to die in the cause of God and to endure thousands
of torments for His sake and to become disgraced in His path,
become as easy as breaking a small straw. One is pulled towards
God without knowing who is pulling. One is carried about by a
hidden hand, and to do God's Will becomes the purpose of one's
life. At this stage God appears very close, as He has said:

$$ وَنَحْنُ اَقْرَبُ اِلَيْهِ مِنْ حَبْلِ الْوَرِيْدِ (ق ١٧) $$

We are closer to him than his jugular vein (50:17).

In that condition the lower relationships of a person fall away
from him, as ripe fruit falls away automatically from the branch of
a tree. His relationship with God deepens and he draws far away
from all creation and is honoured with the word and converse of
God. The doors of access to this stage are as wide open today as
they were at any time, and Divine grace still bestows this bounty
upon those who seek it, as He did before. But this is not achieved
by the mere exercise of the tongue, and this door is not opened
by vain talk and boasts. There are many who seek but there are
few who find. Why is that so? It is because this stage demands
true earnestness and true sacrifice. Mere words mean nothing in
this context. To step faithfully onto the fire from which other
people run away is the first requirement of this path. Boasts avail
nothing; what is needed is practical zeal and earnestness. In this
context God, the Glorious, has said:

وَاِذَا سَاَلَكَ عِبَادِیْ عَنِّیْ فَاِنِّیْ قَرِیْبٌ اُجِیْبُ دَعْوَةَ
الدَّاعِ اِذَا دَعَانِ فَلْیَسْتَجِیْبُوْا لِیْ وَلْیُؤْمِنُوْا بِیْ لَعَلَّهُمْ
یَرْشُدُوْنَ ۔ (البقرة ۱۸۷)

When My servants enquire from thee concerning Me, tell them I am close. I respond to the call of the supplicant when he calls on Me. So should they seek Me through their supplications and have firm faith in Me, that they may be rightly guided (2:187).

SECOND QUESTION

What is the State of Man after Death?

The state of man after death is not a new state, only his condition in this life is made manifest more clearly in the next life. Whatever is the true condition of a person with respect to his beliefs and actions, righteous or otherwise, in this life, remains hidden inside him and its poison or its antidote affects his being covertly. In the life after death it will not be so; everything will manifest itself openly. One experiences a specimen of it in a dream. The prevailing condition of the body of the sleeper makes itself manifest in his dream. When he is heading towards high fever he is apt to see fire and flames in his dream, and if he is sickening due to influenza or a severe cold he is apt to find himself floating about in water. Thus, whatever the body is heading for becomes visible in a dream. So one can understand that the same is the way of God with regard to the afterlife. As a dream transmutes our spiritual condition into a physical form, the same will happen in the next life. Our actions and their consequences will be manifested physically in the next life, and whatever we carry hidden within us from this life will all be displayed openly on our countenances in the next life. As a person observes diverse types of manifestations in his dreams but is not conscious that they are only manifestations, and deems them as realities, the same will happen in the next life. Through such manifestations, God will display a new power, a power which is perfect, complete and absolute as He is All Powerful. If we were not to call the conditions of the next life manifestations and were to say that they would be a new creation by Divine power, that would be perfectly correct.

God has said:

فَلَا تَعْلَمُ نَفْسٌ مَّآ أُخْفِيَ لَهُمْ مِّنْ قُرَّةِ أَعْيُنٍ ۔ (السجدة:١٨)

No virtuous one knows what bliss is kept hidden from him, as a reward for that which he used to do (32:18). Thus God has described all those bounties as hidden, the like of which is not to be found in this world. It is obvious that the bounties of this world are not hidden from us and we are familiar with milk, pomegranates and grapes etc. which we eat here. This shows that the bounties of the next life are something else and have nothing in common with the bounties of this life, except the name. He who conceives of the conditions of paradise in the terms of the conditions of this life has not the least understanding of the Holy Quran.

In interpreting the verse that we have just cited, our lord and master, the Holy Prophet, peace and blessings of Allah be upon him, has said that heaven and its bounties are such as no eye has seen, nor has any ear heard, nor have they been conceived by the mind of man; whereas we see the bounties of this world and hear of them and their thought also passes through our minds. Now when God and His Messenger describe them as something strange, we would depart altogether from the Holy Quran if we were to imagine that in heaven we shall be given the same milk which is obtained in this life from cows and buffaloes, as if herds of milch cattle would be kept in heaven and there will be numerous beehives in the trees of heaven from which angels will procure honey and pour it into streams. Have these concepts any relationship with the teaching that says that those bounties have never been witnessed in this world, and that they illumine the souls and foster our understanding of God and provide spiritual nourishment? They are described in physical terms but we are told that their source is the soul and its righteousness.

Let no one imagine that the verse of the Holy Quran cited below indicates that the dwellers of paradise, on observing these bounties, will recognise them that they had been bestowed these bounties aforetime also, as Allah, the Glorious has said:

وَبَشِّرِ الَّذِيْنَ اٰمَنُوْا وَعَمِلُوا الصّٰلِحٰتِ اَنَّ لَهُمْ جَنّٰتٍ
تَجْرِيْ مِنْ تَحْتِهَا الْاَنْهٰرُ كُلَّمَا رُزِقُوْا مِنْهَا مِنْ
ثَمَرَةٍ رِّزْقًا قَالُوْا هٰذَا الَّذِيْ رُزِقْنَا مِنْ قَبْلُ وَ
اُتُوْا بِهٖ مُتَشَابِهًا - (البقرة:٢٦)

Give glad tidings to those who believe and work perfect righteousness that they will inherit Gardens beneath which rivers flow. Whenever they are provided with fruits therefrom, which they will have already tasted in the life of the world, they will exclaim: This is what we were given before, because they will find that those fruits resemble the fruits which they have already tasted (2:26). It is not to be supposed from the wording of this verse that on beholding the bounties of paradise the dwellers of paradise will discover that they are the same bounties which had been bestowed upon them in their previous life. This would be a great mistake and would be contrary to the true meaning of the verse. What God Almighty has said here is that those who believe and work righteousness, build a paradise with their own hands, the trees of which are their faith and the streams of which are their righteous actions. In the hereafter also they will eat of the fruits of this paradise, only those fruits will be sweeter and more manifest. As they will have eaten those fruits spiritually in this world, they will recognize them in the other world and will exclaim: These appear to be the same fruits that we have already eaten; and they will find that those fruits resemble the fruits that they had eaten before in this world. This verse clearly proclaims that those people who were nurtured in this life on the love of God will be given the same nurture in physical shape in the hereafter. As they will have tasted the delight of love already in this life and would be aware of it, their souls would recall the time when they used to remember their True Beloved in corners, in solitude and in the darkness of night and used to experience its delight.

In short, there is no mention in this verse of material food. If it should strike anyone that as the righteous would have been given this spiritual nourishment in their life in this world it could not be said that it was a bounty that no one had seen or heard of in the world, nor had it been conceived by the mind of man; the answer would be that there is no contradiction here, as this verse does not mean that the dwellers of paradise would be bestowed the bounties of this world. Whatever they are bestowed by way of comprehension of the Divine are the bounties of the hereafter, a specimen of which is given to them in advance to stimulate their eagerness.

It should be remembered that a godly person does not belong to the world, that is why the world hates him. He belongs to heaven and is bestowed heavenly bounties. A man of the world is given worldly bounties, and a man of heaven is bestowed heavenly bounties. Thus it is true that those bounties are hidden from the ears and hearts and eyes of the worldly; but he whose worldly life suffers death and who is given a drink of the spiritual cup which he will drink in a physical form in the hereafter, will then recall having partaken of it in his previous life. It is true, however, that he will consider the eyes and ears of the world as unaware of it. As he was in the world, though he was not of the world, he will also testify that the bounties of heaven are not of the world and that he did not see such a bounty in the world nor did his ear hear of it, nor did his mind conceive it. He saw a specimen of those bounties of the hereafter which were not of this world. They were a presage of the world to come to which he was related and had no connection with the life of this world.

Three Quranic insights concerning the Hereafter

It should be kept in mind that the Holy Quran has set forth three insights with regard to the conditions of the life after death which we now proceed to expound.

First Insight

The Holy Quran has repeatedly affirmed that the life after death is not a new phenomenon and all its manifestations are reflections of this life. For instance, it is said:

وَكُلَّ اِنْسَانٍ اَلْزَمْنٰهُ طَآئِرَهُ فِیْ عُنُقِهٖ وَ نُخْرِجُ

لَهٗ یَوْمَ الْقِیٰمَةِ کِتٰبًا یَّلْقٰهُ مَنْشُوْرًا ﴿بَنِیْۤ اِسْرَآئِیْل ۱۴﴾

Every person's deeds have We fastened firmly to his neck; and on the Day of Judgment We shall make them manifest and shall place them before him in the form of a book which he will find wide open (17:14). In this verse the expression "bird" has been metaphorically employed for actions, because every action, good or bad, flies away like a bird as soon as it is performed and its labour or enjoyment comes to an end; only its heavy or light impress is left on the heart.

The Quran sets forth the principle that every human action leaves its hidden impress upon its author and attracts an appropriate Divine reaction which preserves the evil or the virtue of that action. Its impress is inscribed on the heart and face and eyes and ears and hands and feet of its performer. This is the hidden record which will become manifest in the hereafter.

Concerning the dwellers of heaven, it is said:

$$يَوْمَ تَرَى الْمُؤْمِنِيْنَ وَالْمُؤْمِنٰتِ يَسْعٰى نُوْرُهُمْ$$

$$بَيْنَ اَيْدِيْهِمْ وَ بِاَيْمَانِهِمْ ﴿الحديد: ۱۳﴾$$

On that day thou wilt see the light of the believing men and
the believing women, which is hidden in this world, running
before them and on their right hands manifestly (57:13). At
another place addressing the wrongdoers it is said:

$$اَلْهٰىكُمُ التَّكَاثُرُ. حَتّٰى زُرْتُمُ الْمَقَابِرَ. كَلَّا سَوْفَ$$

$$تَعْلَمُوْنَ. ثُمَّ كَلَّا سَوْفَ تَعْلَمُوْنَ. كَلَّا لَوْ تَعْلَمُوْنَ$$

$$عِلْمَ الْيَقِيْنِ. لَتَرَوُنَّ الْجَحِيْمَ. ثُمَّ لَتَرَوُنَّهَا$$

$$عَيْنَ الْيَقِيْنِ. ثُمَّ لَتُسْـَٔلُنَّ يَوْمَئِذٍ عَنِ النَّعِيْمِ ﴿الكاثر: ۲-۹﴾$$

The desire of increase in wordly possessions beguiles you till
you reach the graves. Do not set your hearts upon the world.
You will soon come to know the vanity of your pursuits; again,
you will soon come to know how mistaken you are in pursuing
the world. If you had possessed the certainty of knowledge you
would surely see hell in this very life. But you will see it with the
certainty of sight in your middle state (*Barzakh*), then you shall
be called to account on the Day of Judgment and the torment will
be imposed on you and you will know hell through your
experience (102:2-9).

Three types of knowledge

In these verses God Almighty has clearly set forth that for the
wicked the life of hell begins in a covert way in this very world,
and if they would reflect they would observe hell in this very life.
Here God Almighty has indicated three types of knowledge,
namely knowledge by certainty of reason, knowledge by certainty

of sight, and knowledge by certainty of experience. This might be illustrated thus. When a person perceives smoke from a distance his mind conceives that smoke and fire are inseparable, and therefore where there is smoke there must be fire also. This would be knowledge by the certainty of reason. Then on a nearer approach he sees the flames of the fire and that is knowledge by the certainty of sight. Should he enter into the fire, that would be knowledge by the certainty of experience. In these verses God Almighty says that knowledge of the existence of hell as a certainty can be acquired in this life through reason, its knowledge through the certainty of sight will be acquired in *Barzakh*, the intermediate state between death and judgment, and on the Day of Judgment that knowledge would become a certainty by experience.

Three conditions

It might be explained at this stage that according to the Holy Quran there are three states of existence.

The *first* is the world, which is called the first creation and is the state of effort. In this world man works good or evil. After resurrection the virtuous will continue their advance in goodness but that would be by the sheer grace of God and would not be the result of any effort of man.

The *second* is the intermediate state which is called barzukh. In Arabic idiom barzukh is something which is situated between two other things. As that state will be between the first creation and the resurrection it is called barzukh. This expression has always been employed for the intermediate state. Thus it comprehends a great hidden testimony in support of the existence of the intermediate state. I have established in my book *Minanur Rahman* that the words of Arabic have issued from the mouth of God and that this is the only language which is the language of the Most Holy God and is the most ancient tongue, and is the fountainhead of all types of knowledge, and is the mother of all languages. and is the first and last throne of Divine revelation. It is the first throne of Divine revelation because Arabic was the language of God that was with God since the beginning. Then that language came down to the world and people converted it into their respective languages. It is the last throne of Divine revelation, inasmuch as the last book of God, which is the Holy Quran, was revealed in Arabic.

Barzukh is an Arabic word which is compounded of *Barra* and *Zakha*, which means that the manner of earning through action has ended and has fallen into a hidden state. *Barzukh* is a state in which the mortal condition of man is dissolved and the soul and the body are separated. The body is buried in a pit and the soul also falls into a sort of pit which is indicated by the expression *Zakha*, because it is no longer able to earn good or evil which it could only do through its relationship with the body. It is obvious that the health of the soul is dependent upon the health of the body. An injury inflicted upon one part of a person's brain causes loss of memory, and an injury occasioned to another part destroys the faculty of reflection and brings about unconsciousness. Similarly a convulsion of the brain muscle, or a swelling or a haemorrhage or morbidity may, by causing obstruction, lead to insensibility, epilepsy, or cerebral apoplexy. Thus our experience teaches us definitely that the soul, divorced from the body, is utterly useless. It is entirely vain to imagine that our soul, without its body, can enjoy any kind of bliss. We might entertain such a fancy but reason lends it no support. We cannot conceive that our soul which is rendered helpless by minor upsets of the body could continue in a perfect condition when its relationship with the body comes to an end altogether. Does not our daily experience teach us that the health of the body is essential for the health of the soul? When one of us reaches extreme old age his soul also falls into dotage. Its store of knowledge is stolen by old age as is said by God, the Glorious, that

$$لِكَيْلَا يَعْلَمَ مِنْ بَعْدِ عِلْمٍ شَيْئًا - (''حج ٠٦)$$

In old age a person arrives at a stage in which, after having acquired much knowledge, he loses it all (22:6). All this observation of ours is proof enough that the soul without the body amounts to nothing. This is reinforced by the thought that if the soul without the body had amounted to anything, it would have been without purpose for God Almighty to set up a relationship between it and a mortal body. Further, it is worthy of note, that God Almighty has created man for limitless progress. Then if the soul is not able to achieve the progress possible in this brief life without the companionship of the body, how can we expect that it would be able, by itself, without the companionship of the body, achieve limitless progress in the hereafter.

All this shows that according to Islamic principles, for the soul to act perfectly, it is necessary for it to enjoy the companionship of a body at all times. On death the soul departs from this mortal body, but in the intermediate state every soul is invested with a body in order to enable it to react to the conditions of that state. That body is not like this physical body, but is prepared from light or from darkness, according to the quality of the person's actions in this life, as if a man's actions serve as a body for the soul in that state. In the Word of God it is repeatedly mentioned that some bodies will be bright and some will be dark. They will be prepared from the light or from the darkness of human actions. This is a fine mystery but is not opposed to reason. A perfect human being can enjoy an illumined body in this very life and there are many instances of this which are experienced in a state of vision. This may be difficult of comprehension by a person of average intelligence, but those who have some experience of the state of vision will not regard such a body as is prepared from human actions as a matter of surprise and improbability, but will duly appreciate this phenomenon.

In short, this body which is acquired according to the condition of one's actions, becomes a source of the recompense of good and evil in the intermediate state. I have experience of this. I have often had experience in a complete state of wakefulness of meeting some persons who had died. and I saw that the bodies of some evil-doers and misguided ones were so dark as if they had been made of smoke. In short, I am personally acquainted with these matters and I affirm emphatically that, as God Almighty has said, every one is invested with a body after death which is either bright or dark. It would be a mistake on the part of man to seek to establish these fine insights through the mere exercise of reason. It should be realised that as the eye cannot discover the taste of something sweet, nor can the tongue behold anything, in the same way the knowledge of the life after death, which can only be acquired through holy visions, cannot be explained fully on the basis of reason. God Almighty has appointed diverse means for acquiring knowledge in this world of that which is unknown. Therefore, it is necessary to seek everything through its proper means. It is only then that it can be discovered.

Another matter that must be kept in mind is that in His Word, God has described as dead those people who are involved in vice and error and has declared the virtuous as alive. The reason for this is that the functions of the lives of those who die in a state of neglect of God, for instance, eating and drinking and indulgence of their passions are cut off, and they have no share of spiritual sustenance. They are truly dead and will be revived only for punishment. As God, the Glorious, has said:

$$ \text{اِنَّهٗ مَنْ يَّأْتِ رَبَّهٗ مُجْرِمًا فَاِنَّ لَهٗ جَهَنَّمَ لَا} $$

$$ \text{يَمُوْتُ فِيْهَا وَ لَا يَحْيٰى ـ (طٰهٰ، ٧٥)} $$

The portion of him who comes to his Lord a sinner is hell; he shall neither die therein nor live (20:75). But those whom God loves do not die with their physical death, for their sustenance is with them.

After *Barzukh* there is the **third** state of resurrection. In that state every soul, good or bad, righteous or disobedient, will be bestowed a visible body. That day has been appointed for the perfect manifestations of God, when every person will get to know the Being of his Lord fully, and everyone will arrive at the climax of his recompense. This should not be a matter for surprise for God has every power and does whatever He wills, as He has said:

$$
\text{اَوَلَمْ يَرَ الْاِنْسَانُ اَنَّا خَلَقْنٰهُ مِنْ نُّطْفَةٍ فَاِذَا هُوَ}
$$

$$
\text{خَصِيْمٌ مُّبِيْنٌ ۚ وَضَرَبَ لَنَا مَثَلًا وَّنَسِيَ خَلْقَهٗ ؕ}
$$

$$
\text{قَالَ مَنْ يُّحْيِ الْعِظَامَ وَهِيَ رَمِيْمٌ ؕ}
$$

$$
\text{قُلْ يُحْيِيْهَا الَّذِيْۤ اَنْشَاَهَاۤ اَوَّلَ مَرَّةٍ ؕ وَهُوَ بِكُلِّ}
$$

$$
\text{خَلْقٍ عَلِيْمٌ ؕ (يٰسٓ: ٧٨ - ٨٠)}
$$

$$
\text{اَوَلَيْسَ الَّذِيْ خَلَقَ السَّمٰوٰتِ وَالْاَرْضَ بِقٰدِرٍ}
$$

$$
\text{عَلٰۤى اَنْ يَّخْلُقَ مِثْلَهُمْ ؕ بَلٰى ۖ وَهُوَ الْخَلّٰقُ الْعَلِيْمُ ؕ}
$$

$$
\text{اِنَّمَاۤ اَمْرُهٗۤ اِذَاۤ اَرَادَ شَيْئًا اَنْ يَّقُوْلَ لَهٗ كُنْ فَيَكُوْنُ ؕ}
$$

$$
\text{فَسُبْحٰنَ الَّذِيْ بِيَدِهٖ مَلَكُوْتُ كُلِّ شَيْءٍ وَّاِلَيْهِ}
$$

$$
\text{تُرْجَعُوْنَ ؕ (يٰسٓ: ٨٢ - ٨٤)}
$$

Does not man know that We have created him from a mere sperm-drop injected into the womb? Then he becomes a persistent disputer. He forgets the process of his own creation but has a lot to say concerning Us. He asks: How shall a person be revived when even his bones have decayed? Who has the power to revive him? Tell them: He, Who created them the first time will revive them. He knows well every type of creation (36:78-80). His power is such that when He determines upon a thing He says concerning it: Be; and it is. Thus Holy is He, in Whose hand is the kingdom over all things. To Him will you all be brought back (36:82-84).

In these verses God, the Glorious, has set forth that nothing is beyond His power. Has He Who created man from a lowly drop not the power to create him a second time?

An ignorant person might object that as the third state, which is the state of resurrection, would arrive after a long period, the state of *barzukh* would only be a sort of lock-up for the good and the bad and this would be purposeless. The answer is that this is a misunderstanding which is due to lack of knowledge. In the Book of God there are two states mentioned for the recompense of the good and the bad, one of which is the state of *barzukh* in which everyone will receive his recompense in a covert manner. The wicked would enter hell immediately on death and the virtuous will find comfort in heaven immediately after death. There are several verses in the Holy Quran to the effect that every person will, immediately on his death, encounter the recompense of his actions. For instance, it is said concerning a righteous one:

$$ \text{قِيْلَ ادْخُلِ الْجَنَّةَ ـ (يٰسٓ ٢٧)} $$

His Lord said to him: Enter thou into paradise (36:27); and concerning a wicked one it is said:

$$ \text{فَرَاٰهُ فِيْ سَوَآءِ الْجَحِيْمِ ـ (الصّٰفّٰت، ٥٧)} $$

This has reference to two friends one of whom was admitted to heaven and the other was condemned to hell. The one who was admitted to heaven was anxious to find out where his friend was. He was shown that his friend was in the midst of hell (37:56). Thus reward and punishment start immediately and those condemned to hell go to hell, and those who are to be admitted to heaven go to heaven. But thereafter there is a day of grand manifestation which has been appointed out of the great wisdom of God. He created man so that He should be recognized through His power of creation. Then He will destroy everything so that He might be recognized through His Supremacy over everything, and then He will gather everyone after bestowing perfect life on them so that He might be recognized through His Power.

Second Insight

The second insight concerning the life after death which the Holy Quran has set forth is that in the hereafter, all the spiritual conditions of this world will be manifested physically, both in the intermediate state and in the resurrection. In this context one verse is:

وَمَنْ كَانَ فِى هٰذِهٖ اَعْمٰى فَهُوَ فِى الْاٰخِرَةِ اَعْمٰى وَاَضَلُّ سَبِيْلًا ۔ بنى اسرائيل: ٧٣،

He who continues blind in this life will be blind in the hereafter and even more astray (17:73). This means that the spiritual blindness of this life will be manifested and felt physically in the hereafter.

In another verse it is said:

خُذُوْهُ فَغُلُّوْهُ ثُمَّ الْجَحِيْمَ صَلُّوْهُ ثُمَّ فِى سِلْسِلَةٍ

ذَرْعُهَا سَبْعُوْنَ ذِرَاعًا فَاسْلُكُوْهُ ۔ الحاقه: ٣١-٣٣

Seize this hellish one and put a collar round his neck and burn him in hell and bind him in a chain the length of which is seventy cubits (69:31-33). These verses show that the spiritual torment of this world will be manifested physically in the hereafter. For instance, the collar of worldly ambition which had bent his head towards the earth will become physically perceptible in the life after death. Similarly the chain of worldly preoccupations will become visible round his feet, and the fire of worldly desires will appear in full blaze.

A vicious person conceals a whole hell of worldly greed and desires inside himself, and perceives the burning sensation of this hell at the time of his failures and frustrations. So when he is cast away from his mortal desires and becomes subject to eternal despair, God Almighty will cause his sorrow to be manifested physically in the shape of fire; as is said:

$$وَحِيْلَ بَيْنَهُمْ وَبَيْنَ مَا يَشْتَهُوْنَ ـ (سبأ ، ٥٥)$$

A barrier will be placed between them and that which they yearn after, and that will be the root of their torment (34:55). The chain of seventy cubits is an indication that a wicked one often attains the age of seventy years and sometimes, leaving aside his years of childhood and extreme old age, he is granted a period of seventy years which he could employ for work wisely and with good sense. But an unfortunate one spends these seventy years caught in the coil of worldly preoccupations and does not desire to be free of them. Thus God Almighty affirms in this verse that the seventy years that such a one spends in worldly pursuits will be manifested as a chain of seventy cubits in the hereafter, one cubit for each year. It must be kept in mind in this connection that God Almighty does not afflict any creature of His with a misfortune from Himself. He merely confronts a person with his own evil deeds.

At another place He has said:

$$إِنْطَلِقُوْآ إِلٰى ظِلٍّ ذِيْ ثَلٰثِ شُعَبٍ لَّا ظَلِيْلٍ وَّلَا يُغْنِيْ$$
$$مِنَ اللَّهَبِ ـ (المرسلت ، ٣١-٣٢)$$

O ye vile and errant ones, proceed towards a shelter which has
three branches, neither affording shade, nor protecting from the
blaze (77:31-32). The three branches mentioned here represent
bestiality, savageness and wild imagination. In the case of those
who do not regulate these faculties and thus convert them into
moral qualities, they will manifest themselves in the hereafter as
three branches of a tree which are bare of leaves and can afford
no shade or protection against fire, so that such people would be
consumed by the fire. As a contrast, God Almighty has said
concerning the dwellers of heaven:

$$\text{يَوْمَ تَرَى الْمُؤْمِنِيْنَ وَالْمُؤْمِنٰتِ يَسْعٰى نُوْرُهُمْ}$$

$$\text{بَيْنَ اَيْدِيْهِمْ وَ بِاَيْمَانِهِمْ ـ (الحديد: ١٣)}$$

On that day thou wilt see the light of the believing men and
believing women, which is kept hidden in this world, running
before them and on their right hands (57:13); and in another
verse it is said:

$$\text{يَوْمَ تَبْيَضُّ وُجُوْهٌ وَّ تَسْوَدُّ وُجُوْهٌ ـ رأل عمرٰن: ١٠٧)}$$

On that day some faces will be bright and others will be dark
(3:107). A third verse sets out:

$$\text{مَثَلُ الْجَنَّةِ الَّتِيْ وُعِدَ الْمُتَّقُوْنَ فِيْهَاۤ اَنْهٰرُ}$$

$$\text{مِّنْ مَّآءٍ غَيْرِ اٰسِنٍ وَ اَنْهٰرٌ مِّنْ لَّبَنٍ لَّمْ يَتَغَيَّرْ}$$

$$\text{طَعْمُهٗ وَاَنْهٰرٌ مِّنْ خَمْرٍ لَّذَّةٍ لِّلشّٰرِبِيْنَ ۚ وَاَنْهٰرٌ}$$

$$\text{مِّنْ عَسَلٍ مُّصَفًّى ـ (مُحَمّد: ١٤)}$$

The Garden promised to the righteous is as if it has rivers of
water that corrupts not; and rivers of milk of which the taste
changes not; and rivers of wine, which do not inebriate, a delight

for those who drink; and rivers of pure honey, which has no impurity (47:16). It is clearly stated here that heaven should be understood as metaphorically comprising inexhaustible streams of these bounties. This means that the water of life which a person of spiritual understanding drinks in this life will be manifested visibly in the hereafter. The spiritual milk by which he is sustained, like a suckling in this life, will become physically visible in heaven. The wine of God's love which inebriated him all the time spiritually in this life, will be manifested in the shape of rivers in heaven. The honey of the sweetness of faith which a person possessing spiritual understanding swallowed spiritually in this world will be manifested and felt physically in heaven. Every dweller of heaven will proclaim his spiritual condition openly through his gardens and rivers. God will unveil Himself on that day for the dwellers of heaven. In short, spiritual conditions will not remain hidden in the hereafter but will be physically visible and perceptible.

Third Insight

The third insight concerning the hereafter is that there will be unlimited progress therein, as God Almighty has said:

$$وَالَّذِيْنَ اٰمَنُوْا مَعَهٗ ۚ نُوْرُهُمْ يَسْعٰى$$

$$بَيْنَ اَيْدِيْهِمْ وَ بِاَيْمَانِهِمْ يَقُوْلُوْنَ رَبَّنَآ اَتْمِمْ$$

$$لَنَا نُوْرَنَا وَاغْفِرْ لَنَا ۚ اِنَّكَ عَلٰى كُلِّ شَىْءٍ قَدِيْرٌ.$$

(التحريم: ۹)

The light of the believers will run before them and on their right hands. They will supplicate: Lord, perfect our light for us and cover us with Thy grace, surely Thou hast power over all things (66:9). Their supplication that their light may be perfected is an indication of limitless progress. It means that when they have arrived at one stage of illumination, they will perceive a higher stage ahead of them and viewing it they will consider the stage in which they are as being inferior and will supplicate for the attainment of the higher stage, and when they arrive at that stage they will perceive a still higher third stage ahead of them and they will supplicate for its achievement. Thus their yearning for constant progress is indicated by the expression: Do Thou perfect our light. In short, this chain of progress will continue indefinitely. There will be no falling away, nor will they be expelled from heaven, but will daily advance further forward.

It may be asked that as they will have entered heaven and all their sins would have been forgiven then what further need would there be for supplicating for forgiveness: The answer is that the true meaning of *maghfirat* (seeking forgiveness), is to suppress and cover up an imperfect or defective condition. Thus the dwellers of heaven will seek the attainment of perfection and their complete absorption in light. Observing a higher condition they will consider their condition defective and would desire its suppression, and then observing a still higher condition they would desire that their lower condition should be covered up and thus they will continuously seek unlimited *maghfirat*. This seeking of *maghfirat* or *istighfar* is sometimes made the basis of adverse criticism of the Holy Prophet, peace and blessings of Allah be upon him. I trust that now it will have become clear that the desire for *maghfirat* is a matter of pride for man. He who is born of woman and does not make *istighfar* his habit, is a worm and not man, he is blind and not seeing, he is unclean and not pure.

In short, according to the Holy Quran, hell and heaven are both reflections of a man's life, and are not something new that comes from outside. It is true that in the hereafter they will be manifested physically, but they will be reflections of the spiritual conditions of man in this life. We do not conceive of heaven as containing material trees, nor of hell as full of brimstone and sulphur. According to Islamic teachings heaven and hell are the reflections of the actions that a person carries out in this world.

THIRD QUESTION

The Object of Man's Life and the Means of its Attainment

Different people, being shortsighted and lacking high resolve, appoint different purposes for their lives and limit themselves to worldly goals and ambitions. But the purpose that God Almighty has appointed for man in His Holy Word is as follows:

$$وَمَا خَلَقْتُ الْجِنَّ وَالْإِنْسَ إِلَّا لِيَعْبُدُونِ (الذاريات:٥٧)$$

I have created men and jinn so that they may know Me and worship Me (51:57). Thus the true purpose of man's life is the worship of God, His understanding and complete devotion to Him.

It is obvious that man is not in a position to appoint the purpose of his own life, for he does not come into the world of his own accord, nor will he depart therefrom of his own will. He is a creature and the One Who created him and invested him with better and higher faculties than those of all other animals, has also appointed a purpose for his life. Whether anyone penetretes to it or not, the purpose of man's creation without a doubt is the worship and the understanding of God and complete devotion to Him. At another place God Almighty has said in the Holy Quran:

$$إِنَّ الدِّينَ عِنْدَ اللهِ الْإِسْلَامُ - (آل عمران:٢٠)$$

$$فِطْرَتَ اللهِ الَّتِي فَطَرَ النَّاسَ عَلَيْهَا .... ذَٰلِكَ الدِّينُ$$

$$الْقَيِّمُ (الرّوم:٣١)$$

The religion which provides true understanding of God and prescribes His true worship is Islam (3:20). Islam is inherent in man's nature and man has been created in accord with Islam. That is the everlasting faith (30:30-31). This means that God has desired that man should devote himself to His worship and obedience and love with all his faculties. That is why He has bestowed on man all the faculties that are appropriate for Islam.

These verses have very wide meaning, a part of which we have set out in the third part of the answer to the first question. Here we wish to state briefly that the true purpose of the internal and external limbs and faculties that have been bestowed on man is the understanding of God and His worship and His love. That is why, despite occupying himself with diverse projects in this life, man does not find his true welfare except in God. Having had great wealth, having held high office, having become a great merchant, having ruled a great kingdom, having been known as a great philosopher, in the end he departs from all these involvements with great regret. His heart constantly rebukes him on his total preoccupation with worldly affairs and his conscience never approves his cunning and deceit and illicit activities. An intelligent person can appreciate this problem in this way also, that the purpose of everything is to be determined by its highest performance beyond which its faculties cannot operate. For instance, the highest function of a bullock is ploughing or irrigation or transportation. Its faculties are not adapted to anything else. Therefore, the purpose of a bullock's life are just these three things. It has no power to do anything else. But when we look into the faculties of man and try to discover what is their highest reach, we find that he seeks after God, the Exalted. He desires to become so devoted to God that he should keep nothing as his own and all that is his should become God's. He shares with the other animals his natural urge towards eating, sleeping etc. In industry some animals are far ahead of him. Indeed the bees extracting the essence of different types of flowers produce such excellent honey that man has not yet been able to match them. It is obvious, therefore, that the highest reach of man's faculties is to meet God, the Exalted. Thus the true purpose of his life is that the window of his heart should open towards God.

Means of the Attainment of Man's purpose

It may be asked how can this purpose be achieved and through what means can a person find God? The very *first* means of achieving this goal is to recognize God Almighty correctly and to believe in the True God. For if the very first step is not right, for instance, if a person believes in a bird, or an animal, or in the elements, or in the issue of a human being, as god, there can be no hope of his treading along the straight path in his further progress towards God. The True God helps His seekers, but how can a dead god help the dead? In this context God the Glorious has set forth an excellent illustration:

$$
\text{لَهٗ دَعْوَةُ الْحَقِّ ۖ وَ الَّذِيْنَ يَدْعُوْنَ مِنْ دُوْنِهٖ لَا}
$$

$$
\text{يَسْتَجِيْبُوْنَ لَهُمْ بِشَيْءٍ اِلَّا كَبَاسِطِ كَفَّيْهِ اِلَى الْمَآءِ}
$$

$$
\text{لِيَبْلُغَ فَاهُ وَمَا هُوَ بِبَالِغِهٖ ۖ وَمَا دُعَآءُ الْكٰفِرِيْنَ}
$$

$$
\text{اِلَّا فِيْ ضَلٰلٍ ـ ﴿الرَّعْد: ١٥﴾}
$$

Unto Him alone is the true prayer, as He has the power to do all things. Those on whom they call beside Him, do not respond to them at all. Their case is like that of one who stretches forth his hand towards water that it may reach his mouth, but it reaches it not. The prayers of those who are unaware of the True God are but a delusion (13:15).

The *second* means is to be informed of the perfect beauty of God Almighty; for the heart is naturally drawn to beauty, the observation of which generates love in the heart. God's beauty is His Unity and His Greatness and His Majesty and His other attributes, as the Holy Quran has said:

قُلْ هُوَ اللّٰهُ اَحَدٌ ـ اللّٰهُ الصَّمَدُ ـ لَمْ يَلِدْهُ وَلَمْ يُوْلَدْ

وَلَمْ يَكُنْ لَّهٗ كُفُوًا اَحَدٌ ـ (الاخلاص: ۲ ـ ۵)

God is One in His being and His attributes and His glory. He has no partner. All are dependent upon Him. He bestows life on every particle. He is the source of grace for everything and is not in need of grace from any. He is neither a son nor a father for He has no equal and no one is like unto Him (112:2-6). The Quran repeatedly draws attention to God's greatness and grandeur and thus impresses upon the minds of men that only such a God can be the desired objective of the heart and not any dead or weak or pitiless or powerless being.

The *third* means of approach to God is knowledge of His beneficence; for beauty and beneficence are the two incentives of love. The beneficient attributes of God are summed up in Surah Fatiha as follows:

اَلْحَمْدُ لِلّٰهِ رَبِّ الْعٰلَمِيْنَ ـ الرَّحْمٰنِ الرَّحِيْمِ ـ مٰلِكِ يَوْمِ الدِّيْنِ ـ

That is to say God creates His servants from nothing, out of perfect Beneficence and His Providence is available to them all the time. He is the support of everything and every type of His beneficence has been manifested for His creatures (1:2-4). His benevolence is without limit as He has said:

وَاِنْ تَعُدُّوْا نِعْمَتَ اللّٰهِ لَا تُحْصُوْهَا ـ (ابرٰهيم: ۳۵)

If you try to count the bounties of Allah you would not be able to number them (14:35).

The *fourth* means of achieving the true purpose of life appointed by God Almighty is supplication, as He has said:

اُدْعُوْنِیْ اَسْتَجِبْ لَکُمْ - (المؤمن:٦١)

Call on Me, I shall respond to you (40:61). We are repeatedly urged to supplicate so that we should find God, not through our power but through God's power.

The *fifth* means of achieving the purpose of life appointed by God Almighty, is striving in His cause; that is to say, we should seek God by spending our wealth in His cause and by employing all our faculties in furthering His cause, and by laying down our lives in His cause and by employing our reason in His cause; as He has said:

وَجَاهِدُوْا بِاَمْوَالِکُمْ وَاَنْفُسِکُمْ فِیْ سَبِیْلِ اللّٰهِ (التوبة:٤١)

وَمِمَّا رَزَقْنٰهُمْ یُنْفِقُوْنَ - (البقرة:٤)

وَالَّذِیْنَ جَاهَدُوْا فِیْنَا لَنَهْدِیَنَّهُمْ سُبُلَنَا - (العنکبوت:٧٠)

Strive in His way with your wealth and your lives and with all your faculties (9:41); and: Whatever We have bestowed upon you of intelligence and knowledge and understanding and art, employ it in Our cause (2:4). We surely guide along Our ways those who strive after Us (29:70).

The *sixth* means of achieving this purpose has been described as steadfastness, meaning that a seeker should not get tired or disheartened and should not be afraid of being tried, as God has said:

اِنَّ الَّذِیْنَ قَالُوْا رَبُّنَا اللّٰهُ ثُمَّ اسْتَقَامُوْا تَتَنَزَّلُ عَلَیْهِمُ الْمَلٰئِکَةُ اَلَّا تَخَافُوْا وَلَا تَحْزَنُوْا وَاَبْشِرُوْا بِالْجَنَّةِ الَّتِیْ کُنْتُمْ تُوْعَدُوْنَ۔ نَحْنُ اَوْلِیٰٓؤُکُمْ

فِى الْحَيوةِ الدُّنْيَاوَفِى الْأَخِرَةِ ۔ (لخم السجدة:۳۱-۳۲)

Upon those who affirm: God is our Lord, and turn away from false gods and are steadfast, that is to say, remain firm under trials and calamities, descend angels, reassuring them: Fear not nor grieve, and be filled with happiness; and rejoice that you have inherited the joy that you had been promised. We are your friends in this life and in the hereafter (41:31-32). These verses indicate that steadfastness wins the pleasure of God Almighty. It is true, as has been said, that steadfastness is more than a miracle. The perfection of steadfastness is that when one is encircled by calamities and life and honour and good name are all in peril in the cause of Allah, and no means of comfort are available, so much so, that even visions and dreams and revelation are suspended by God as a trial, and one is left helpless among terrible dangers, at such a time one should not lose heart nor retreat like a coward nor let one's faithfulness be put in doubt in the least. One should not let one's sincerity and perseverance be weakened, one should be pleased with one's disgrace; one should be reconciled to death; one should not wait for a friend to lend one his support in order to keep one firm; nor seek glad tidings from God because of the severity of the trial. One should stand straight and firm despite one's helplessness and weakness and lack of comfort from any direction. Come what may one should present oneself for sacrifice and should be completely reconciled to divine decrees and one should exhibit no restlessness nor utter any complaint, right till the end of the trial. This is the steadfastness which leads to God. This is that the perfume of which still reaches us from the dust of Messengers and Prophets and Faithful ones and Martyrs.

This is also indicated in the supplication:

اِهْدِنَا الصِّرَاطَ الْمُسْتَقِيمَ۔ صِرَاطَ الَّذِينَ اَنْعَمْتَ عَلَيْهِمْ ۔(الفاتحة:۷۔۶)

Guide us along the path of steadfastness, the path that attracts Thy bounties and favours and by treading along which one wins Thy pleasure (1:6-7). Another verse also indicates the same:

رَبَّنَآ أَفْرِغْ عَلَيْنَا صَبْرًا وَّ تَوَفَّنَا مُسْلِمِينَ ۔ (الاعراف:۱۲۷)

Lord, send down on us steadfastness in this time of trial and cause us to die in a state of submission to Thee (7:127). It should be realised that at a time of misfortunes and hardships God Almighty causes a light to descend upon the hearts of those He loves; by being strengthened with this light they face those misfortunes with great serenity; and out of the sweetness of faith they kiss the chains that fetter them. When a godly person is afflicted and the signs of death become manifest, he does not start a contention with his Beneficent Lord that he might be delivered from that condition, inasmuch as to persist in a supplication for security in such a condition means fighting God's decree and is inconsistent with complete submission. A true lover goes further forward under misfortunes and, holding life as nothing at such a time, and saying goodbye to it, submits completely to the will of God and seeks only His pleasure. Concerning such people God Almighty has said:

وَ مِنَ النَّاسِ مَنْ يَّشْرِي نَفْسَهُ ابْتِغَآءَ مَرْضَاتِ اللّٰهِ
وَاللّٰهُ رَءُوْفٌ بِالْعِبَادِ ۔ (البَقَرَة: ۲۰۸)

He whom God loves offers his life in the cause of God in return for God's pleasure. Such people win the compassion of God (2:208). This is the spirit of steadfastness through which one meets God. Let him who will understand.

The *seventh* means of achieving the purpose of life is to keep company with the righteous, and to observe their perfect example. One of the needs for the advent of prophets is that man naturally desires a perfect example, and such an example fosters zeal and promotes high resolve. He who does not follow an example becomes slothful and is led astray. This is indicated by Allah, the Glorious, in the verse:

كُوْنُوْا مَعَ الصّٰدِقِيْنَ - (التوبة : ١١٩)

صِرَاطَ الَّذِيْنَ اَنْعَمْتَ عَلَيْهِمْ - (الفاتحه: ٧)

Keep company with the righteous (9:119); and in the verse: Guide us along the path of those upon whom Thou hast bestowed Thy favours (1:7) that is to say, you should keep company with the righteous and learn the ways of those who have been the recipients of grace before you.

The *eighth* means of achieving the purpose of life are visions and true dreams and revelation. As the path that leads to God Almighty is a difficult one and is studded with misfortunes and hardships and it is possible that a person might go astray while treading along this unfamiliar path and might begin to despair and stop going forward, the mercy of God desires to keep comforting him and encouraging him and augmenting his zeal and eagerness. So it is His way that from time to time He comforts such people with His Word and His revelation and makes it manifest to them that He is with them. Thus they are strengthend and go forward eagerly on this journey. He has said:

لَهُمُ الْبُشْرٰى فِى الْحَيْوةِ الدُّنْيَا وَ فِى الْاٰخِرَةِ - (يُونس:٦٥)

For them there are glad tidings in this life and in the hereafter (10:65). The Holy Quran has set forth several other means for the achievement of the purpose of life, but we refrain from setting them down here out of consideration of time.

FOURTH QUESTION

The Operation of the Practical Ordinances of the Law in this Life and the Next

We have already stated that the effect of the true and perfect Divine law upon man's heart in this life is that it lifts him from a savage condition and converts him into a human being, and thereafter invests him with high morals, and finally makes him godly. One of the effects of the practical ordinances of the law is that a person who follows the true law progressively recognises the rights of his fellow beings and exercises his faculties of equity, and benevolence, and true sympathy, on their proper occasions. Such a one shares with his fellow beings, according to their respective ranks, the bounties with which God has favoured him, like knowledge, understanding, wealth and means of comfort. He sheds his light like the sun upon the whole of mankind, and like the moon, acquiring light from God, conveys it to others. Being illumined like the day he shows the paths of virtue and goodness to others, and like the night he covers up their weaknesses and provides comfort for those who are weary. Like the sky he provides shelter under his shade for everyone who is in need, and pours down the rain of grace at its proper time. Like the earth, out of utter humility, he becomes like a floor for everyone's comfort and gathers them close to afford them security, and offers them diverse types of spiritual fruits. Thus, he who adheres to the perfect law discharges his obligations to God and to his fellow creatures to the utmost. He loses himself in God and becomes a true servant of His creatures. This is the effect of the practical ordinances of the law on his life here.

Their effect in the hereafter is that a person who adheres to them will observe his spiritual relationship with God as a manifest reality. The service that he rendered to God's creatures out of his love for God, which was stimulated by his faith, and his yearning for righteous action, will be manifested to him as the trees and rivers of paradise. In this context, God Almighty has said:

وَالشَّمْسِ وَضُحٰهَا۔ وَالْقَمَرِ اِذَا تَلٰهَا۔ وَالنَّهَارِ اِذَا جَلّٰهَا۔
وَالَّيْلِ اِذَا يَغْشٰهَا۔ وَالسَّمَآءِ وَمَا بَنٰهَا۔ وَالْاَرْضِ وَمَا طَحٰهَا۔
وَنَفْسٍ وَّمَا سَوّٰهَا۔ فَاَلْهَمَهَا فُجُوْرَهَا وَتَقْوٰهَا۔ قَدْ اَفْلَحَ مَنْ
زَكّٰهَا۔ وَقَدْ خَابَ مَنْ دَسّٰهَا۔ كَذَّبَتْ ثَمُوْدُ بِطَغْوٰىهَآ۔
اِذِانْبَعَثَ اَشْقٰهَا۔ فَقَالَ لَهُمْ رَسُوْلُ اللّٰهِ نَاقَةَ اللّٰهِ وَ
سُقْيٰهَا۔ فَكَذَّبُوْهُ فَعَقَرُوْهَا فَدَمْدَمَ عَلَيْهِمْ رَبُّهُمْ بِذَنْبِهِمْ فَسَوّٰهَا۔
وَلَا يَخَافُ عُقْبٰهَا۔ (الشمس ٢: ١٦)

We call to witness the sun and its light; and We call to witness the moon when it follows the sun and obtains its light from it and conveys it to people; and We call to witness the day when it manifests the light of the sun and shows up the paths; and We call to witness the night when it darkens and envelops everything within itself; and We call to witness the heaven and the purpose for which it has been created; and We call to witness the earth and the purpose for which it has been spread out like a floor; and We call to witness the human soul and its quality which makes it equal to all these other things; that is to say all those qualities which are found dispersed among the other bodies that have been mentioned are all comprehended in the soul of the perfect man. As these bodies serve man in diverse ways, the perfect man performs all that service by himself. Then He says: That one will be delivered from death and will attain salvation who purifies his soul, that is to say, who serves God's creatures out of his devotion to God like the sun and the moon and the earth.

It should be kept in mind that in this context life means life eternal, which will be bestowed upon perfect man. This is an indication that the fruit of conforming to the practical ordinances of the law will be the eternal life of the next world, which will be sustained for ever by the vision of God. Then it is said that he who corrupts his soul and does not acquire the qualities for which he was bestowed appropriate capacities and goes back after spending an unclean life, shall be ruined and shall despair of life eternal. This is illustrated by the event of the she-camel of Allah, which was hamstrung by a wretched one of the tribe of Thamud and was prevented from drinking at its fountain. This is an indication that the soul of man is the she-camel of God which He bestrides, meaning that the heart of man is the place of Divine manifestations. The water of the she-camel is the love and understanding of God which sustain it. When the Thamud hamstrung the she-camel of God and prevented it from having its drink, they were overtaken by God's chastisement and He cared not how their dependants would fare. Thus would be ruined one who corrupts his soul and prevents it from taking spiritual nourishment and does not desire to foster it (91:2-16).

The Philosophy of the Oaths of the Holy Quran

There is a deep philosophy in God's calling the sun and the moon etc. to witness. Some of our opponents, out of their lack of knowledge, criticise God for calling to witness created things. As their intelligence is earthly and not heavenly they fail to appreciate true insights. The purpose of taking an oath is that the one who takes an oath puts forward a testimony in support of his claim. A person who has no witness of his claim calls God to witness, for He knows what is hidden and He is the foremost witness in every controversy. Such a person puts forward the testimony of God by taking an oath in His name, meaning thereby that if God does not thereafter chastise him, that would be proof that God has confirmed the truth of his claim. It is, therefore, not permissible for a person to take the oath of any created thing, for no created thing possesses knowledge of the unseen, nor has it the power to punish one who takes a false oath. In these verses, God calling various phenomena to witness is not the same thing as a person taking an oath. Divine manifestations are of two types. One, those that are obvious and concerning which there is no controversy. Secondly, there are those Divine manifestations which are inferential concerning which people differ and can fall into error. By calling to witness the obvious phenomena, God Almighty's purpose is to establish by their evidence His inferential manifestations.

It is obvious that the sun and the moon and the day and the night and the heaven and the earth, possess the respective characteristics that we have mentioned, but everyone is not aware of the characteristics possessed by the human soul. Thus, God has set forth His obvious manifestations as witnesses for the purpose of explaining His inferential manifestations. It is as if He says: If you are in doubt with regard to the qualities with which the human soul is invested, then reflect upon the sun and the moon and the other phenomena cited which obviously possess these qualities. You know that man is a microcosm that comprises a tiny representation of the pattern of the universe. As it is clear that the great bodies of the macrocosm possess these qualities and provide benefits for God's creatures, then how can man, who ranks above all those bodies, be without those qualities? That is not so. Indeed, like the sun, man possesses the light of knowledge and reason whereby he can illumine the world. Like the moon he receives the light of vision and revelation from the Divine and conveys it to others who have not yet arrived at the highest stage of human progress. Then how can you say that prophethood is a false notion and that all prophethoods and purported Divine laws and books are only the imposture and selfishness of certain human beings. You observe how all paths are lit up and the heights and depressions become distinct when the day dawns. In the same way perfect man is the day of spiritual light, by his advent every path becomes clearly distinguishable. He points out the right path, for he himself is the bright day of truth and righteousness. Similarly, you observe how the night accommodates the weary and how the labourers, after working hard during the day, sleep in the gracious lap of the night and rest from their labours. The night also covers up all defects and imperfections. In the same way, the perfect servants of God come to provide comfort for people and the recipients of revelation relieve all wise people of extreme effort. Through them great problems of insight are easily resolved. Also Divine revelation covers up the defects of human reason and, like the night, does not let its faults to become known, inasmuch as wise people correct their mistakes on their own in the light of revelation, and thus through the blessings of God's holy revelation save themselves from being exposed. That is the reason why no Muslim philosopher offered the sacrifice of a rooster to an idol as was done by Plato. Plato was misled as he was deprived of the light of revelation and despite being a great philosopher he perpetrated such a stupid and hateful act. The following of our lord and master the Holy Prophet, peace and blessings of Allah be upon him, safeguarded the Muslim philosophers against such stupid and unholy practices. This shows how Divine revelation covers up, like the night, the deficiencies of the wise.

You are also aware that the perfect servants of God provide, like heaven, shelter for every weary one. His prophets and the recipients of His revelation pour down the rain of their beneficence like the sky, and they also possess the qualities of the earth. Diverse types of trees of high knowledge spring forth from their fine souls, from the shade and flowers and fruits of which people derive benefit. Thus, this visible law of nature which is displayed before our eyes is a witness of the hidden law whose testimony God Almighty has cited in these verses by way of oaths. Reflect, therefore, how full of wisdom is the word that is found in the Holy Quran and which issued from the mouth of an unlettered dweller of the desert. Had it not been the Word of God, the wise ones and those who are called highly educated, being confronted with this fine insight, would not have made it the subject of criticism. It is a common experience that when a person is unable to appreciate something on the basis of his finite reason he criticises that which is based on wisdom and his criticism becomes proof that that point of wisdom is above and beyond the reach of average minds. That is why those who are accounted wise raised an objection against this phenomenon; but now that the mystery has been resolved no reasonable person will criticise it but will derive pleasure from it.

The Holy Quran has, at another place, recited such an oath for the purpose of citing an instance of the law of nature in support of the phenomenon of revelation, and has said:

وَالسَّمَاۤءِ ذَاتِ الرَّجْعِ ۔ وَالْاَرْضِ ذَاتِ الصَّدْعِ ۔

اِنَّهٗ لَقَوْلٌ فَصْلٌ ۔ وَّمَا هُوَ بِالْهَزْلِ ۔ (الطارق: ۱۲-۱۵)

We call to witness the heaven that sends down rain and the earth that sprouts diverse types of vegetation with the help of such rain, that the Quran is God's word and His revelation, and that it decides between truth and falsehood and is not vain talk, that is to say, it has not been revealed out of time and has come like seasonable rain (86:12-15).

Here God Almighty has set forth a well known law of nature in support of the truth of the Holy Quran, which is His Word. It is a matter of common observation that at a time of need rain comes down from heaven and that the vegetation of the earth all depends upon rain. When rain is held back then gradually the wells also run dry, so that the water in the earth also depends upon rain from heaven. That is why in the rainy season the level of the water in the wells also rises, the reason for which is that heavenly water exercises a pull upon earthly water. The same is the relationship between divine revelation and human reason. Divine revelation is heavenly water and reason is earthly water which receives sustenance from heavenly water. When heavenly water, that is to say, divine revelation, is held back, the earthly water also dries up gradually. That is the reason why, when a long time passes and no recipient of revelation appears on the earth, the reason of the wise is corrupted, as earthly water is corrupted and dries up. To appreciate this phenomenon it would be enough to cast a glance at the condition of the world immediately before the advent of the Holy Prophet, peace and blessings of Allah be upon him. As six hundred years had passed after the time of Jesus, and no recipient of revelation had appeared during the interval, the whole world had been corrupted. The history of every country shows that before the advent of the Holy Prophet, peace and blessings of Allah be upon him, falsehood had become current throughout the world. Why did this happen? This happened because divine revelation had been held back for a long time and the kingdom of heaven had fallen into the hands of human reason alone. No one is unaware of the corruption in which the people were involved by following defective reason. Thus, when the rain of revelation did not descend for a period, the water of reason dried up.

So in these oaths God Almighty draws attention to this firm and eternal law of nature and calls for reflection upon it that all the vegetation of the earth depends upon the water of heaven. Thus, for the hidden law that governs divine revelation, the obvious law of nature is a witness. Then try to derive benefit from the testimony of this witness and do not make reason alone your guide, for it is not a water that can continue without heavenly water. As it is a characteristic of heavenly water that it pulls up the water of all the wells, whether it falls directly into a well or not, in the same way, when a recipient of divine revelation appears in the world then, whether a wise person follows him or not, reason is illumined and clarified to a degree not witnessed before. People begin to search for the truth and their faculty of reflection is stirred up from the unseen. Thus, all this upsurge of reason and of the heart is initiated by the blessed advent of the recipient of divine revelation and the waters of the earth are pulled up by it. So, when you find that everyone has started a search for religion and an upsurge has stirred earthly waters, then rise up and be warned and know for certain that heavy rain has fallen from heaven and that the water of divine revelation has fallen upon a human heart.

FIFTH QUESTION

Sources of Divine Knowledge

The comprehensiveness with which the Holy Quran has dealt with this subject cannot be set forth at this stage for want of time. We shall, therefore, confine ourselves to a concise statement by way of illustration.

The Holy Quran has drawn attention to three types of knowledge: knowledge by way of certainty of inference, knowledge by way of certainty of sight, and knowledge by way of certainty of experience. As we have already explained knowledge by certainty of inference is that a thing should be known not directly but through something through which it can be inferred, as by observing smoke we infer the existence of fire. We do not see the fire, but see the smoke and because of it we believe in the existence of the fire. Then if we see the fire, this, according to the Holy Quran, would be certainty by sight. If we were to enter into the fire, our knowledge would have the quality of certainty by experience. We have set out all this already and we refer our listeners and readers to that exposition.

It should be known that the source of the first type of knowledge, that is to say knowledge by the certainty of inference, is reason and information. God Almighty sets out in the Holy Quran that the dwellers of hell will affirm:

قَالُوْالَوْكُنَّا نَسْمَعُ اَوْنَعْقِلُ مَاكُنَّافِیْۤ اَصْحٰبِ

السَّعِيْرِ - (المُلك ٠ ۱۱)

That if they had exercised their reason and had approached the consideration of religion and doctrine sensibly, or had listened to and read with attention the speeches and writings of the wise and the scholars, they would not have been condemned to hell (67:11). This is in accord with another verse where it is said:

لَا يُكَلِّفُ اللهُ نَفْسًا إِلَّا وُسْعَهَا . (البقرة: ٢٨٧)

That is to say, God Almighty does not require human beings to accept anything that is beyond their intellectual capacity, and only sets forth such doctrines as are comprehensible by men, so that His directives should not impose upon man that which he is not able to bear (2:287). These verses also indicate that one can obtain the certainty of knowledge by inference through one's ears also. For instance, we have not visited London and have only heard of it from those who have visited it, but then can we imagine that all of them might have told a lie? Or, we did not live in the time of Emperor Alamgir, nor did we see him, but can we have any doubt that Alamgir was one of the Moghul emperors? How did we arrive at that certainty? The answer is, through the continuity of hearing about him. Thus, there is no doubt that hearing also carries one's knowledge to the stage of certainty by inference. The books of the Prophets are also a source of knowledge through hearing, provided there should be no contradiction in the account that is heard. But if a book claims to be revealed and there are fifty or sixty versions of it, some of which contradict others, then even if a party might have held that only two, or three, or four of them were accurate and that the rest were spurious or fabricated, this would be no kind of proof which could be made the basis of any sure knowledge. All those books would be rejected as unreliable on account of their contradiction and could not be held to be a source of knowledge; for knowledge is only that which bestows a sure understanding, and a collection of contradictions can bestow no certain understanding.

The Holy Quran is not confined merely to knowledge gained through continuity of hearing, it contains well reasoned arguments which carry conviction. Not one of the doctrines and principles and commandments that it sets forth is sought to be imposed merely by authority; as it has explained, they are all inscribed in man's nature. It is called a Reminder as is said:

وَ هٰذَا ذِكْرٌ مُّبٰرَكٌ ۘ ۔ (الانبیاء: ٥١،)

Meaning that the Blessed Quran does not set forth anything that is new but is a reminder of that which already exists in man's nature and in the book of nature (21:51). At another place it is said:

لَآ اِكْرَاهَ فِى الدِّيْنِ ۔ (البقرة: ٢٥٧،)

Meaning that Islam does not try to inculcate anything by compulsion, but sets forth reasons in support of everything (2:257). The Quran possesses a spiritual quality that enlightens the hearts, as it says:

شِفَآءٌ لِّمَا فِى الصُّدُوْرِ ۔ (يُونس: ٥٨،)

It is a healing for that which afflicts the minds (10:58). Thus it is not merely a book that has been transmitted through generations, but comprises reasoned arguments of a high degree and is charged with shining light.

Thus, intellectual arguments which have a sound basis undoubtedly lead a person to the certainty of knowledge by inference. This is indicated in the following verses:

اِنَّ فِىْ خَلْقِ السَّمٰوٰتِ وَ الْاَرْضِ وَ اخْتِلَافِ الَّيْلِ
وَ النَّهَارِ لَاٰيٰتٍ لِّاُولِى الْاَلْبَابِ ۔
الَّذِيْنَ يَذْكُرُوْنَ اللّٰهَ قِيٰمًا وَّ قُعُوْدًا وَّ عَلٰى جُنُوْبِهِمْ
وَ يَتَفَكَّرُوْنَ فِىْ خَلْقِ السَّمٰوٰتِ وَ الْاَرْضِ ۚ رَبَّنَا مَا

خَلَقْتَ هٰذَا بَاطِلاً سُبْحٰنَكَ فَقِنَا عَذَابَ النَّارِ ـ رال عمرن: ۱۹۱-۱۹۲

When wise and sensible persons reflect on the structure of the earth and the heavenly bodies and ponder over the alternation of the day and the night, they discover therein reasons in support of the existence of God. Thereupon they seek divine help for greater enlightenment and they remember God standing, and sitting, and lying on their sides, whereby their intellects are sharpened and their pondering over the structure of the earth and heavenly bodies impels them to affirm that this firm and orderly system could not have been created in vain but is a manifestation of divine attributes. Thus, confessing the Godhead of the Creator of the universe, they supplicate: Lord Thou art Holy above being denied and being attributed imperfect qualities. Safeguard us, therefore, against the fire of hell; meaning that a denial of God is very hell itself and that all comfort and delight proceed from Him and from His recognition. He who is deprived of the recognition of God abides in hell in this very life (3:191-192).

The Nature of Human Conscience

Human conscience is also a source of knowledge which has been named human nature in the Book of God, as is said;

فِطْرَتَ اللهِ الَّتِيْ فَطَرَ النَّاسَ عَلَيْهَا ـ رالرُومِ: ۳۱

Follow the nature designed by Allah, the nature according to which He has fashioned mankind (30:31). What is the impress of that nature? It is to believe in God as One, without associate, Creator of all, above birth and death. We have described conscience as a source of knowledge by certainty of inference though, apparently, in this case the mind does not travel from one type of knowledge to another as it does on the observation of smoke to the inference of fire, and yet here also there is a very fine type of transference, which is that God has invested everything with a particular quality which cannot be described in words, but towards which one's mind is directed immediately upon observing that thing or contemplating it. That quality is inherent in everything as smoke is inherent in fire. For instance, when we contemplate the Being of God Almighty and consider what it should be, whether God should be born like us and should suffer and die like us, instantly thereat our heart is tormented and our conscience trembles and indignantly rejects any such idea and cries out that the God, upon Whose powers all our hopes are centered, must be free from all defects and must be Holy and Perfect and Powerful. The moment we think of God, we perceive a perfect relationship between God and Unity, even exceeding that which subsists between fire and smoke. Therefore, the knowledge that we gain through conscience is knowledge at the stage of certainty through inference. But there is another stage about it which is called knowledge through certainty of sight. That is a degree of knowledge when there is no intermediary between us and that of which we have gained knowledge. For instance, when we perceive a good or bad smell through our sense of smell, or perceive the sweetness or saltness of something through our sense of taste, or perceive the warmth or coldness of anything through our sense of feeling, all such knowledge is, as it were, certainty through sight.

With regard to the hereafter our knowledge arrives at the degree of certainty by sight when we receive direct revelation and hear the voice of God through our ears, and behold the true and clear visions of God with our eyes. Without a doubt we are in need of direct revelation for the purpose of achieving such perfect understanding for which our hearts hunger and thirst in our beings. If God Almighty has not provided the means of such comprehension for us in advance then why has He created this hunger and thirst in our hearts? Can we be content that in this life, which is our only measure for the hereafter, we should believe in the true and perfect and mighty and living God only on the basis of tales and stories, or should depend upon understanding or reason alone, which understanding is still defective and incomplete? Do not the hearts of true lovers of God desire that they should enjoy the delight of converse with the Beloved, and should those who have given up everything in the world for the sake of God and have devoted their hearts and lives to Him, be content with repining in a dim light without beholding the coutenance of that Sun of Truth? Is it not true that an affirmation by the Living God: I am present; bestows such a degree of understanding compared with which the self conceived books of all the philosophers amount to nothing at all? What can those so-called philosophers who are themselves blind teach us? In short, if God Almighty designs to bestow perfect understanding upon His seekers then He has certainly kept open the way of converse with them. In this context God, the Glorious, has taught us the supplication in the Holy Quran:

$$ \text{اِهْدِنَا الصِّرَاطَ الْمُسْتَقِيْمَ ـ صِرَاطَ الَّذِيْنَ اَنْعَمْتَ عَلَيْهِمْ (الفاتحة:٦-٧)} $$

Guide us along the path of those upon whom Thou hast bestowed Thy favours (1:6-7). Here by divine favours is meant heavenly knowledge by way of revelation and visions that are bestowed directly upon man. At another place it is said:

$$ \text{اِنَّ الَّذِيْنَ قَالُوْا رَبُّنَا اللهُ ثُمَّ اسْتَقَامُوْا تَتَنَزَّلُ} $$

$$ \text{عَلَيْهِمُ الْمَلَآئِكَةُ اَلَّا تَخَافُوْا وَلَا تَحْزَنُوْا وَاَبْشِرُوْا} $$

$$ \text{بِالْجَنَّةِ الَّتِيْ كُنْتُمْ تُوْعَدُوْنَ ـ (رحم السجدة: ٣١)} $$

Upon those who, having believed in God, continue steadfast, descend God's angels reassuring them: Fear not, nor grieve, and rejoice in the paradise that you have been promised (41:31). Here

it is clearly stated that the righteous servants of God receive
revelation from God at times of fear and grief and angels descend
upon them to reassure them. At another place it is said:

$$لَهُمُ الْبُشْرٰى فِى الْحَيٰوةِ الدُّنْيَا وَ فِى الْاٰخِرَةِ ـ ر يونس: ٦٥،$$

The friends of God receive glad tidings in this life through
revelation and converse with God and will also have the same
experience in the hereafter (10:65).

Meaning of Revelation

It should be kept well in mind that revelation does not mean
that an idea should arise in the mind of a person who sets himself
to ponder over a thing as, for instance, a poet having thought out
half a verse seeks the other half in his mind and his mind suggests
the other half. This is not revelation but is the result of reflection,
in accordance with the law of nature. When a person reflects
upon something good or bad, a corresponding idea arises in his
mind. For instance, one person who is pious and truthful
composes verses in support of truth, and another one, who is
wicked and vicious, supports falsehood in his verses and abuses
the righteous. Both these would, no doubt, write a certain
number of verses, and it is quite possible that the verses of the
one who is the enemy of the righteous and supports falsehood
might be better than the verses of the other one, on account of his
greater practice in writing poetry. So, if the arising of an idea in
the mind should be accounted as revelation, a vile poet who is the
enemy of truth and of the righteous and writes in opposition to
the truth and has recourse to imposture, would be called a
recipient of divine revelation. Many novels are written in
excellent style and set forth altogether false but continuous well
arranged tales. Then would these stories be designated as
revelation? If revelation were to mean merely an idea arising in
one's mind, a thief would also be called a recipient of revelation,

for an expert thief often thinks out surprising ways of theft and robbery, and many clever plans of robbery and murder pass through his mind. Would all these unclean projects be called revelation? Indeed not. Such is the thinking only of those who are not aware of the true God Who comforts the hearts of His servants with His converse and bestows the understanding of spiritual knowledge upon those who are not familiar with it.

What then is revelation? It is the living and powerful converse of the Holy and Mighty God with a chosen servant of His, or with one whom He designs to make His elect. When this converse starts in an adequate and satisfactory manner, being altogether free from the darkness of false concepts, and is not composed merely of a few inadequate and meaningless words, and is full of delight and wisdom and grandeur, then it surely is the word of God with which He designs to comfort His servant and to manifest Himself to him. Sometimes revelation is vouchsafed to a person by way of trial and is not equipped with full blessings. In such a case the recipient is put on his trial at this elementary stage so that having tasted somewhat of revelation he should order his life along the lines of those who are true recipients of revelation, in default of which he would encounter frustration. If he does not adopt the ways of the truly righteous he is deprived of the fullness of this bounty and is left only with vain boasting.

Millions of the virtuous have been recipients of revelation, but they were not of equal standing in the estimation of God. Indeed, even the holy Prophets of God, who are recipients of divine revelation at the highest level, are not equal in rank, as God Almighty has said:

$$ تِلْكَ الرُّسُلُ فَضَّلْنَا بَعْضَهُمْ عَلَى بَعْضٍ ـ (البقرة: ٢٥٤) $$

Of these Messengers some have We exalted above others (2:254). This shows that revelation is pure divine grace and is not evidence of exaltation. Exaltation is according to the degree of truth, sincerity, and faithfulness of the recipient, which is known only to God. If revelation possesses all its blessed conditions it is also one of the fruits of such qualities. There is no doubt that if revelation takes the form that the recipient submits a question and God responds to it, and there is a sequence between question and answer, and the revelation is characterized by divine majesty and light, and comprehends knowledge of the unseen and true understanding, it is truly the word of God. It is necessary that divine revelation should be like a dialogue between two friends. Likewise, when God communes with His servant, and when the servant enquires concerning any matter, and in response to that he hears an address, which is sweet and full of linguistic excellence, in matters, in which his mind had not interpolated in the least, that dialogue and revelation can certainly be understood as Word of God. Such servant of Allah, is indeed, great in the sight of Allah; but this exeptional high status of being recipient of the Word of God, as a special favour from Him, which has the quality of absolute clarity and purity, which is not bestowed upon anyone but those, who continuously progress in faith, dedication and righteous deeds. Also there is something extra to it (of spiritual nature) which is beyond us to describe. True and holy revelation displays many wonders of the Godhead. Very often a brilliant light is generated and along with it a majestic and shining revelation is vouchsafed. What could be a greater bounty than this that a recipient of revelation should hold converse with the Being Who is the Creator of the heavens and the earth. God can be seen in this world only through converse with Him.

This does not include the condition of a person from whose tongue an idle word, or sentence or verse proceeds unaccompanied by any dialogue. Such a person is under trial by God, for God sometimes tries a slothful and neglectful servant of His in this manner that a sentence or a statement issues from his heart or tongue and he becomes a blind person not knowing whence the statement has proceeded, whether from God or from Satan. Such a one should implore *istighfar* in respect of such an experience. But if a righteous and virtuous servant of God should experience unobstructed dialogue with the Divine and should hear bright, and delicious, and meaningful, and wise, and majestic divine utterances in a state of complete wakefulness in the shape of question and answer at least ten times, that is to say he put a question and God replied to it and then in complete wakefulness he made another submission and God made answer to it, and he made another humble supplication and God replied to that. This should have happened ten times. If in the course of such dialogue God should accept his prayers and should instruct him in excellent insights and should inform him of coming events and should honour him repeatedly with His clear dialogue, such a one should be deeply grateful to God Almighty and should be more devoted to Him than anyone else, because God, of His pure grace, has chosen him from among His servants and has made him the heir of those faithful ones who have passed on before him. This bounty is most rare and is the height of good fortune. For him on whom it is bestowed everything else is utterly without value.

A characteristic of Islam

Islam has always produced persons of this rank. It is Islam alone in which God approaches a servant and holds converse with him and speaks inside him. He builds His throne in the heart of such a one and pulls him from inside towards heaven. He bestows upon him all the bounties that were bestowed on those before him. It is a pity that the blind world does not realise how far a person can reach in nearness to God. They do not step forward themselves, and if another one does so, he is either declared a disbeliever or he is deified and is put in the place of God. Both these are great wrongs which proceed from one extreme or the other. A wise one should not lack high resolve and should not persist in the denial of such an exalted rank being conferred on anyone, and should neither denigrate such a one nor deify him. When a person attains such high rank, God Almighty manifests such relationship with him as if He covers him up with the mantle of His Godhead and such a one becomes a mirror for beholding God. That is why the Holy Prophet, peace and blessings of Allah be upon him, said: He who has seen me has seen God. This is the last stage in the spiritual progress of man in which he is bestowed full satisfaction.

The Speaker is Honoured with Divine Converse

I would be guilty of doing great wrong to my fellow beings if I were not to declare at this stage that divine bounty has bestowed upon me the status which I have just defined and has honoured me with the kind of converse the features of which I have just set out in detail, so that I should bestow sight upon the blind and should guide the seekers of the One Who has been so far lost, and should give to those who accept the truth the good news of that holy fountain of which many speak but which few find. I wish to assure the listeners that the God, meeting with Whom is the salvation and eternal welfare of man, cannot be found without following the Holy Quran. Would that the people were to see that which I have seen, and were to hear that which I have heard, and should lay aside mere tales and should run to the truth. The cleansing water which removes all doubt, that mirror through which that Supreme Being can be seen, is converse with the Divine that I have just mentioned. Let him whose soul seeks the truth arise and search. I tell you truly that if souls are charged with true seeking and hearts develop true thirst, people would search for that way and would seek that path. How can that way be discovered, and how can the intervening veil be removed? I assure all seekers that it is Islam alone which conveys the good news of that path. All other people have since long sealed up divine revelation. Be sure, however, that this seal is not imposed by God, but is an excuse that is put forward by man on account of his privation. Be sure that as it is not possible that we should be able to see without eyes, or should be able to hear without ears, or should be able to speak without a tongue, in the same way it is not possible that without the help of the Quran we should be able to behold the countenance of the True Beloved. I was young and am now old but I have not encountered anyone who has quaffed the cup of this visible understanding except out of this holy fountain.

The Source of Perfect Knowledge is Divine Revelation

Dear ones, no one can fight God's designs. Be sure that the source of perfect knowledge is divine revelation which is bestowed on the holy prophets of God. Therefore God, Who is the ocean of grace, did not design that divine revelation should be sealed up for the future and the world should thus be destroyed. The doors of His revelation and converse are always open. If you seek them along their proper ways you will find them easily. The water of life has come down from heaven and has stopped at its proper place. What must you do, so that you might drink of it? You should, by some means or the other, arrive at that fountain and should put your mouth to it so that you might be filled with the water of life. The entire good fortune of a person consists in this that he should run in the direction in which he perceives that light, and should adopt the way in which he discovers a sign of the Friend Who has been lost. You have observed that light always descends from heaven and falls upon the earth. In the same way the true light of guidance also descends from heaven. Man's own devices and his own conjectures cannot bestow true understanding upon him. Can you behold God without His manifestation? Can you see in the dark without the help of heavenly light; If you can you may perhaps see in this case also. But our eyes, though in perfect condition, depend on heavenly light; and our ears, though they can hear perfectly, depend upon the air which circulates under divine direction. That god is not true who is silent and leaves everything to our conjectures. The Perfect and Living God is He Who manifests Himself on His own. At this time also He has designed to disclose His own Being. The windows of heaven are about to open, the day is about to dawn. Blessed are those who should rise up and seek the True God, the One Who is not overtaken by any calamity, the brilliance of Whose Glory is never dimmed. It is said in the Holy Quran:

$$ اَللّٰهُ نُوْرُ السَّمٰوٰتِ وَالْاَرْضِ (النُّور: ۳۷) $$

meaning that all the light of the heavens and the earth proceeds from God and lights up everything. He is the Sun that bestows light upon the sun, and He is the life of all the animates in the earth. He is the True Living God. Blessed are those who accept Him (24:36).

The third source of knowledge is certainty through experience, that is to say, all the hardships and calamities and sufferings that are experienced by the Prophets and the righteous at the hands of their opponents, or that are imposed upon them by Divine decree. Through these hardships and sufferings all the commandments of the law and its directions that were comprehended by the human mind intellectually, appear in practical shape and become experience, and by being developed by practical exercise arrive at their climax, and the person concerned himself becomes a perfect code of Divine guidance. All the moral qualities like forbearance, retribution, endurance, mercy etc. which hitherto pervaded the mind and heart theoretically, become part of the personality through practical experience and make their impress upon the total personality of the sufferer, as God the Glorious has said:

وَلَنَبْلُوَنَّكُمْ بِشَىْءٍ مِّنَ الْخَوْفِ وَالْجُوعِ وَنَقْصٍ مِّنَ
الْاَمْوَالِ وَالْاَنْفُسِ وَالثَّمَرٰتِ وَبَشِّرِ الصّٰبِرِيْنَ ۙ
الَّذِيْنَ اِذَآ اَصَابَتْهُمْ مُّصِيْبَةٌ قَالُوْآ اِنَّا لِلّٰهِ وَاِنَّآ
اِلَيْهِ رٰجِعُوْنَ ؕ اُولٰٓئِكَ عَلَيْهِمْ صَلَوٰتٌ مِّنْ رَّبِّهِمْ
وَرَحْمَةٌ ٞ وَاُولٰٓئِكَ هُمُ الْمُهْتَدُوْنَ ؕ (الْبَقَرَة : ١٥٧–١٥٨)

لَتُبْلَوُنَّ فِيْۤ اَمْوَالِكُمْ وَاَنْفُسِكُمْ ۟ وَلَتَسْمَعُنَّ مِنَ الَّذِيْنَ
اُوْتُوا الْكِتٰبَ مِنْ قَبْلِكُمْ وَمِنَ الَّذِيْنَ اَشْرَكُوْۤا اَذًى
كَثِيْرًا ؕ وَاِنْ تَصْبِرُوْا وَتَتَّقُوْا فَاِنَّ ذٰلِكَ مِنْ عَزْمِ
الْاُمُوْرِ ۔ (أل عمرٰن : ١٨٧)

We shall surely try you with somewhat of fear and hunger and loss of wealth and lives and of the fruits of your labour, that is to say, you will suffer all this at the hands of your enemies or by virtue of Divine decree. Then give glad tidings to the steadfast, who, when a misfortune overtakes them, do not lose heart but say: Surely to Allah we belong and to Him shall we return. It is these on whom are blessings from their Lord and mercy, and it is these who are rightly and perfectly guided (2:156-158). These verses indicate that there is no virtue in the knowledge that is confined to the mind and heart. True knowledge is that which emerges from the mind and regulates and trains all the limbs, and manifests in practice all the store of memory. Thus knowledge is strengthened and fostered through its impress being imposed on all the limbs by practical experience. No type of knowledge, however elementary, arrives at its climax without practice. For instance, we have always known that baking bread is perfectly easy and involves no great art. All that is needed is that after kneading the flour and preparing the dough, we should divide it into balls of proper size and pressing each ball between our hands should spread it out and place it on a properly heated pan, and move it about till it is heated into bread. But this is only our academic boast. When without experience we start the process of baking, our first difficulty is to prepare the dough in its proper condition so that it neither becomes too hard nor remains too soft. Even if we succeed in preparing the dough after much effort and weariness, the bread that we bake will be part burnt and part unbaked with lumps all over of irregular shape, despite our observation of the process of baking over a period of half a century. Thus relying upon our bare knowledge which we have never practised, we would suffer a loss of a quantity of flour. If such is the case of our academic knowledge in elementary matters, then how can we rely solely on our knowledge without any practical experience in matters of great import? Thus God Almighty teaches us in these verses that the sufferings which He imposes upon us are a means of perfecting our knowledge through experience.

He has then warned us: You will surely be tried in respect of your possessions and your persons, that is to say, people will plunder your wealth and will kill you; and you will surely suffer many hurtful things at the hands of Jews and Christians and of those who set up partners with Allah; but if you show fortitude and restrain yourselves, that indeed would be evidence of high resolve (3.187). The purport of all these verses is that only that knowledge is beneficial which has been tested by experience, and the knowledge that is merely academic and has not been the subject of experience is without beneficence.

As wealth is multiplied by commerce, in the same way knowledge arrives at its spiritual climax through practical experience. Thus practical experience is the principal means of perfecting knowledge and bestows a light upon knowledge. The ultimate certainty of knowledge is achieved through experience of every part of it. That is what happened in Islam. God Almighty provided the Muslims with the opportunity to illustrate whatever they were taught in the Quran in their practice and thus to become filled with its light.

Two Phases of The Life of the Holy Prophet

That is why God Almighty divided the life of the Holy Prophet, peace and blessings of Allah be upon him, into two phases; one phase of hardship and calamities and sufferings, and the other of victory; so that during the phase of sufferings those high moral qualities might be demonstrated which come into play at such times, and during the phase of victory and authority those high moral qualities might be illustrated which cannot be displayed in the absence of authority. Thus both these types of qualities were perfectly illustrated in the life of the Holy Prophet, peace and blessings of Allah be upon him, by his passing through both these phases and conditions. During the period of trials in Mecca, which extended over thirteen years, the Holy Prophet, peace and blessings of Allah be upon him, demonstrated in practice all the high qualities which a perfectly righteous person should exhibit at such a time, such as trust in God, perfect serenity under sufferings, steady and eager carrying out of duties and fearless courage. Observing his steadfastness many of the disbelievers believed in him and thus testified that it is only the one who has complete trust in God who can display such steadfastness and endurance of suffering.

During the second phase, that is to say the phase of victory, authority and prosperity, he demonstrated such high qualities as forbearance, forgiveness, benevolence and courage, so that a large number of the disbelievers believed in him through witnessing his exercise of those high qualities. He forgave those who had persecuted him, granted security to those who had expelled him from Mecca, bestowed great wealth upon those among them who were in need and having obtained authority over his bitter enemies, forgave them all. Witnessing his high morals many of them testified that such qualities could only be demonstrated by one who comes from God and is truly righteous. That is how all the rancour that his enemies had entertained against him over a long period was washed out of their hearts in an instant. His greatest quality was the one that is set out in the Holy Quran in the following words:

قُلْ اِنَّ صَلَاتِیْ وَنُسُکِیْ وَمَحْیَایَ وَمَمَاتِیْ لِلّٰهِ رَبِّ الْعٰلَمِیْنَ ۔ (الانعام: ۱۶۳)

Tell them: My worship and my sacrifices and my living and my dying are all wholly for Allah (6.163). This means that the whole purpose of his life was to demonstrate the glory of God and to provide comfort for His creatures so that through his constant suffering of death they might procure life. No one should be misled by the mention of his death in the cause of God and for the good of His creatures, into thinking that he had at any time (God forbid) contemplated destroying himself, imagining like the ignorant and the insane, that his suicide would be of benefit to others. He was entirely free from any such stupid line of thinking and was wholly opposed to it. The Holy Quran esteems anyone who is guilty of self destruction as a great offender, liable to severe chastisement, as it says:

وَلَا تُلْقُوْا بِاَیْدِیْکُمْ اِلَی التَّهْلُکَةِ ۔ (البقرة: ۱۹۵)

that is to say, do not commit suicide and do not become the cause of your own destruction (2:196). It is obvious that if X suffers from pain in the stomach, it would be futile for Y to break his own head out of pity for X. That would be no virtuous deed but only needless suffering through stupidity. In the circumstances it would have been virtuous on the part of Y to minister to X in an appropriate and useful manner, for instance, by procuring medical advice and the required medicines for him. His breaking his own head would do no good to X. It would be the infliction of needless suffering upon a noble part of his own body. In short the true meaning of the verse cited above is, that the Holy Prophet, peace and blessings of Allah be upon him, out of true sympathy, had devoted his life to labour for the welfare of mankind and through supplications and exhortations and enduring their persecution and by every proper and wise means had laid down his life and sacrificed his comfort in this cause; as God the Glorious has said:

$$لَعَلَّكَ بَاخِعٌ نَّفْسَكَ اَلَّا يَكُوْنُوْا مُؤْمِنِيْنَ ـ (الشعرآء:٤)$$

$$فَلَا تَذْهَبْ نَفْسُكَ عَلَيْهِمْ حَسَرٰتٍ ـ (فاطر:٩)$$

Haply thou wilt risk death grieving that they do not believe (26:4); and: Let not thy soul waste itself in sighing after them (35:9). Thus the wise way of laying down one's life in the service of one's people is to endure hardship in their service in accord with the beneficial law of nature, and to spend one's life working out appropriate projects to that end, and not to strike one's head with a stone because of the perilous situation of one's people resulting from their errors or afflictions, or to depart this life after swallowing two or three grains of strychnine imagining that through this absurd device one would open the way of salvation for one's people. This is not a manly method, but is a feminine tendency. It has always been the way of faint-hearted people that finding themselves unable to endure hardship they run towards suicide. Whatever explanation may be offered in respect of it there can be no doubt that such action is sheer folly.

Again, it is obvious that the endurance of hardship and nonresistance to an enemy on the part of a person who never had the opportunity to take revenge, cannot be accounted a moral quality. for it is not known how would he have behaved if he had had an opportunity of taking revenge. Unless a person passes through hardships and then achieves authority and prosperity his true qualities cannot be manifested. It is obvious that a person whose whole life is spent in a state of weakness, indigence, and helplessness, enduring persecution all the time, and who is never in a position of authority and power and prosperity, cannot be adjudged as possessing high moral qualities. If he has had no opportunity of taking part in a battle it cannot be determined whether he is brave or a coward. We cannot make any estimate of his character as we do not know how would he have treated his enemies, if he had overcome them, or how would he have spent his wealth if he had become prosperous. Would he have hoarded it or would he have distributed it among the people; and if he had been present in the field of battle would he have run away or would he have behaved as a brave fighter? In the case of the Holy Prophet, peace and blessings of Allah be upon him, Divine favour and grace afforded him full opportunity for the manifestation of his moral qualities. He displayed generosity, bravery, meekness, forbearance and equity on their appropriate occasions to such perfection that it would be a vain effort to look for their match in any other person. In both phases of his life, in weakness and power, indigence and prosperity, he demonstrated to the whole world to what high degree he comprehended all the moral qualities. There is no high moral quality for the exercise of which God Almighty did not afford him an opportunity. All excellent moral qualities like bravery, generosity, steadfastness, forbearance, meekness, etc., were in his case so clearly established that it is not possible to seek his equal. It is also true that those who had carried their persecution of him to the extreme and had designed the destruction of Islam, were not left unpunished by God. To forego chastisement in their case would have amounted to the destruction of the righteous under the heels of their enemies.

The Purpose of The Wars of The Holy Prophet

The purpose of the wars of the Holy Prophet, peace and blessings of Allah be upon him, was not to cause needless bloodshed. The Muslims had been expelled from their ancestral homes, many innocent Muslim men and women had been martyred, and still the wrongdoers were not prepared to restrain themselves, and continuously obstructed the progress of Islam. In these circumstances the Divine law of security demanded the safeguarding of the persecuted ones against total destruction. Therefore, those who had drawn the sword were opposed with the sword. Thus those wars were directed towards rooting out the mischief of those who were bent upon murder and were aimed at repelling evil. They took place at a time when the wrongdoers were bent on the ruin of the righteous. In these circumstances, if Islam had not had recourse to measures of self defence, thousands of innocent women and children would have been slaughtered and an end would have been put to Islam.

It is a great error on the part of our opponents that they imagine that revealed guidance must under no circumstances inculcate resistance to the enemy and should always demonstrate its love and mercy by way of meekness and gentleness. Such people imagine that they display great reverence for God, the Lord of Honour and Glory, by attributing to Him only the qualities of gentleness and tenderness. But those who are given to reflection and pondering can easily perceive that such people are involved in gross and obvious error. A contemplation of the Divine law of nature clearly shows that it certainly is pure mercy. But that mercy does not manifest itself by way of gentleness and tenderness in all circumstances. Out of pure mercy, like an expert physician, it sometimes administers a sweet draught to us and at other times it prescribes a bitter medicine for us. Divine mercy deals with us as each of us deals mercifully with his body. There can be no doubt that each of us loves his whole body and if anyone wishes to pull out a single hair of ours we are much annoyed with him. Yet despite the fact that the love that we bear towards our body is distributed over the whole of it, and all our limbs are dear to us, and we do not desire the loss or hurt any of them, it is clear that our love for every one of our limbs is not of the same degree and quality. In fact, the love of our principal limbs upon which largely depends the carrying out of our purposes, prevails over our hearts. Similarly in our estimation the totality of our limbs is far greater than our love for any particular limb. Thus when we are confronted with a situation in which the security of a superior limb depends upon wounding or cutting or breaking an inferior limb, we reconcile ourselves to such an operation. We are grieved at the wounding or cutting of a limb that is dear to us, but through the apprehension lest the disorder of the inferior limb should operate to destroy a superior limb, we are reluctantly reconciled to its cutting. This illustration should help us to realize that when God observes that His righteous servants are in peril of being destroyed at the hands of the worshippers of falsehood and that this would lead to great disorder He manifests His appropriate design, whether from heaven or from earth, for the safeguarding of the righteous and for the putting down of disorder; for as He is Merciful, He is also Wise.

All praise belongs to Allah the Lord of the Universe.